Chi

Books of the Year

Selected and Annotated by
JULIA ECCLESHARE

Andersen Press · London

British Library Cataloguing in Publication data

Children's books of the year.
1989
1. Children's books. Bibliographies. Serials
I. National Book League
011 .625054 05

ISBN 0 86264 262 0

Published by Andersen Press in association with Book Trust in 1989
62-65 Chandos Place
London WC2

ISBN 0 86264 262 0

The selected titles in this publication are available for hire as
a Book Trust touring exhibition. Contact the Head of Exhibitions,
Book Trust, Book House, 45 East Hill, London SW18 for details.

Cover illustration is by Susan Varley

Typeset by Print Origination (NW) Ltd, Liverpool L37 8EG
Printed in Italy by Grafiche AZ, Verona

CHILDREN'S BOOKS OF THE YEAR 1989

Key to symbols used
P   Paperback

1989 is Julia Eccleshare's fifth year as selector of *Children's Books of the Year*. She has been Children's Books Editor for the *Times Literary Supplement* (1974-78) and was Fiction Editor for Puffin Books (1978-79) and for Hamish Hamilton (1979-84).

She now works as a freelance reviewer, is married with three young children and lives in London.

Children's Books of the Year 1989

INTRODUCTION

For better or worse, books for children are fairly and squarely in the public eye. With the coming of the 1988 Education Reform Act and the laying down of a core curriculum which includes English, what reading is for and various ways of how it may best be learned and developed have been ordained. Emphasis has rightly been placed on the literary and language experience that each child should encounter rather than on what they should know or be able to achieve at any given time. Stress lies firmly on reading for meaning and enjoyment, whether at the initial stages of learning or as fluency and confidence increase.

This is most encouraging. All kinds of literature are recognised as important - particular mention is made of poetry, fairy tales and folk stories and non-fiction, as well, of course, as many different kinds of fiction. As long as teachers, parents, librarians and publishers also commit themselves to understanding that reading is first and foremost for meaning and enjoyment in all these different genres, then writing for children will continue to match the high standards of the past.

In this year's selection there are books which show that high standards of writing can be found in what is published for readers of all ages, stages and tastes. Sadly, it is very much the gilt on some rather stale gingerbread. In all areas there is a sense that many books are being written too quickly, published too quickly - without enough attention being paid to a detailed editing of the text or to finding illustrators whose work enhances the story - and sold too quickly, which means that they have a brief life and, if not successful enough, a quick death.

Set against these less than satisfactory books it is especially pleasing to find the ones on which thought, time and attention have been spent. As in previous years the quality of many of the books which are available for those beginning to 'read' pictures and listen to the accompanying story is particularly high. Prizes are by no means the only or even necessarily the best yardstick for measuring the potential success of a book, but *Can't You Sleep, Little Bear?* (51) by Martin Waddell and Barbara Firth deserves all the accolades it has received for the sureness of its text, its illustrations and the integration of the two. It is also a book which speaks directly and with understanding to the very young audience for whom it was conceived.

Other picture books stand out for different reasons. Concern for our environment is not new but, with the notable exception of Michael Foreman's *Dinosaurs and all that Rubbish* it has not been a very common theme in picture books. This year's selection includes several books which touch on themes of conservation. Helen Cowcher's *Rainforest*(13) stands out for its ability to convey a powerful message within an interesting and attractive medium.

At all other stages, whether they are taking the first faltering steps or reading fluently and voraciously, readers can find books in this selection which will show just why reading is such an important and versatile skill. Beginning readers will laugh at *Mrs Jolly's Joke Shop* (65) by Allan Ahlberg and Colin McNaughton. Fluent readers may be moved to tears by Nina Bawden's *Keeping Henry* (90). Teenage readers will learn how hard decisions can be in *A Begonia for Miss Applebaum* (180) by Paul Zindel, while they may find relief in Anne Fine's witty exploration of a serious theme in *Goggle-Eyes* (148).

There are, in fact, few subjects which remain unexplored in this year's selection. Anyone of any age can find out everything they need to know about how things work in David Macaulay's encyclopedic *The Way Things Work* (286). Not everyone wants to take an active part in a sport but Steve Pinder's and Rob Steen's *Sportswatching* (303) makes comprehending almost any physical activity comparatively straightforward.

The selection of poetry books, folk stories and fairy stories also offers something for every taste. Michael Harrison's *Splinters* (217) is an unusual collection of rhymes which make their point succinctly and satisfyingly. Poetry is thriving in schools and has been given a central role in the guidelines for the teaching of English. Further information about poets and how poetry is written can be found in *There's a poet behind you* . . . edited by Morag Styles and Helen Cook (A & C Black) and in *Did I hear you write?* by Michael Rosen (Andre Deutsch).

Speaking and listening, writing, and reading, are the central planks in the English curriculum. Well written books, in all genres, are needed to provide the necessary source material. These are the books which will get children listening; they are the ones which will get children reading and encourage them to go on doing so; and they are the ones which will enable them to learn to write fluently. Let's have more of them.

1988/89 PRIZEWINNING
CHILDREN'S BOOKS

1987 Carnegie Medal
PRICE, Susan *The Ghost Drum* Faber
1987 Kate Greenaway Medal
HADITHI, Mwenye *The Crafty Chameleon* Hodder & Stoughton
1988 The Children's Book Award (Federation of Children's Book Groups)
DAHL, Roald *Matilda* Cape
1989 Guardian Children's Fiction Award
McCAUGHREAN, Geraldine *A Pack of Lies* Oxford University Press
1988 Kurt Maschler Award
BROWNE, Anthony *Alice's Adventures in Wonderland* Julia MacRae
1988 Mother Goose Award
FUGE, Charles *Bush Vark's First Day Out* Macmillan
1989 Parents Magazine Best Book For Babies Award
GRINDLEY, Sally *Wake Up Dad* Simon & Schuster
1988 Signal Poetry Award
MOLE, John *Boo to a Goose* Peterloo Poets
1988 Smarties Book Prize
Grand Prix and under 5's winner
WADDELL, Martin illus. FIRTH, Barbara *Can't You Sleep Little Bear?* Walker Books
6-8 years winner
HILL, Susan illus. BARRETT, Angela *Can It Be True?* Hamish Hamilton
9-11 years winner
WHISTLER Theresa & Brixworth Primary School *Rushavenn Time*
1988 T.E.S. Information Book Award
Junior - THOMSON, Ruth & FAIRCLOUGH, Chris *Making a Book* Franklin Watts
WATTS, Barrie *Conker* A. & C. Black
Senior - SCHLIDEAT, Valerie BROWN, Pam *Martin Luther King* Exley Publications
1988 T.E.S. School Book Award
COLES, Mike ed. *Active Science* Collins Educational
1988 Tir Na n-Og Award
Best Fiction Award - HYWYN, Gwenno *Tydi Bywyd yo Boen!* Gwasg Gwynedd
Best Book of the Year Award - PRWIG, Dafydd *Yr Atlas Cymraeg* Gwasg Gwynedd
The English Award - LUCAS, Celia *Steel Town Cats* Tabb House
1988 Whitbread Award (Children's Books)
ALLEN, Judy *Awaiting Developments* Julia MacRae
1988 The Kathleen Fidler Award in association with Book Trust Scotland

MORGAN, Charles *Flight of the Solar Duck* Blackie
1989 The Earthworm Children's Book Award administered by Friends of the Earth
ALLEN, Judy *Awaiting Developments* Julia MacRae
1989 The Science Book Prize administered by C.O.P.U.S & sponsored by the Science Museum
MACAULAY, David & ARDLEY, Neil *The Way Things Work* Dorling Kindersley
All prizes correct at the time of going to press

These picture books have been selected for their pictures, their texts or, ideally, for their skill in truly integrating the two. Encouraging children to look at pictures and follow the stories that they tell is the first step towards enjoying books.

1
AARDEMA, Verna
(reteller)
Rabbit Makes a Monkey
of Lion
illustrated by Jerry
Pinkney
Bodley Head
1989 £6.95 32pp
0 370 31329 1

Jerry Pinkney's lush and dramatic illustrations turn this lively folk tale into a vibrant picture book which powerfully evokes the interaction of the animals within the jungle. The story tells of how Rabbit outwits Lion over the matter of some honey in the Calabash tree. Verna Aardema's text is linguistically rich and very readable.

2
AGGREY, James
The Eagle That Would
Not Fly
illustrated by Wolf
Erlbruch
Magi
1988 £5.95 32pp
1 870271 90 4

When an eagle is caught by a collector and put among his chickens it starts to live like a chicken and to think like a chicken. It doesn't yearn for the freedom of the skies, instead it is content to live quietly in the farmyard. It is only when a naturalist shows it the brilliance of the sun that its brave eagle heart is stirred and it flies off to freedom. Written to remind Black people of their true nature it contains a strong message for everyone about individuality and fulfilment.

3
AHLBERG, Janet
AHLBERG, Allan
Starting School
Viking Kestrel
1988 £6.95 36pp
0 670 81688 4

Absolutely everything that happens when you start school can be found in this sensitive picture book. Through the wholly integrated text and artwork the reader follows six children from their first apprehensive day to a triumphant Christmas play and the end-of-term Christmas party. Nothing is glossed over and each child is given sufficient character to make their responses to every situation convincingly different.

4
ANNO, Mitsumasa
Upside-Downers
Macmillan
1988 £6.50 32pp
0 333 46646 2

Mitsumasa Anno's pictures and text demand interactive looking. Printed the right way up or upside down they challenge the normal notions about looking at books. But, *Upside-Downers* has an internal logic of its own and following the ingenious story is fun while also offering thought-provoking speculation about what is up and what down.

5
BAKER, Alan
One Naughty Boy
Andre Deutsch
1989 £5.95 24pp
0 233 98093 8

With the help of some clever peepholes Alan Baker builds up a richly textured countryside in which one naughty boy teases two sleepy badgers, while three sly foxes hunt four playful rabbits and so on until ten angry bees turn the tables and chase one muddy boy, shown falling splashily backwards into a pond. Alan Baker's observation of the countryside is close and his details of animals, birds, flowers, fruits and fungi demand and repay careful looking.

6
BAKER, Jeannie
Where the Forest Meets
the Sea
Julia MacRae
1988 £6.95 32pp
0 86203 317 9

Both text and illustrations to *Where the Forest Meets the Sea* have a lyrical and haunting quality. The story tells of a small boy's trip to a far off rain forest - a place which has remained unchanged for over a hundred million years. Exploring, the boy senses the history of the place. Anything or anyone could still be alive within its dark and secret recesses. Through the use of exquisite collages made from all manner of materials, Jeannie Baker's artwork allows readers to enter that same mysterious world.

7
BLATHWAYT, Benedict
Bear's Adventure
Julia MacRae
1988 £5.95 32pp
0 86203 330 6

Bear's Adventure is a simple, satisfying and nicely turned story about a bear who is left on the beach by mistake and his resulting adventures. The illustrations are clear, each one showing the details of the particular environment in which Bear finds himself - a crowded sea bed, a cosy ship's cabin, a bustling quayside.

8
BRADMAN, Tony
Not Like That, Like This!
illustrated by Joanna
Burroughes
Methuen
1988 £5.95 32pp
0 416 06342 X

In demonstrating to Thomas how *not* to get his head caught in the railings, Dad does just that. One old lady, two men with their dogs,

three park keepers, four people jogging, five boys on their bikes and so on, try to rescue Dad. At last a great big fire engine and the ten firemen on board succeed. Lots of action and bold and bright pictures make this a visually exciting counting book.

9
BROWN, Marc
Arthur's Baby
Piccadilly
1988 £5.50 32pp
1 85340 019 X

The opening of *Arthur's Baby* shows just why parents should not make the kind of statements which they do. 'We have a surprise for you,' said Mother and Father. 'Is it a bicycle?' asked Arthur. Poor Arthur, the surprise is not a bicycle but the news of a forthcoming baby. Marc Brown's amusing and understated text and his comic semi-animal, semi-human illustrations make a good picture book as well as covering many of the anxieties and pleasures that having a new brother or sister can bring.

10
BROWN, Ruth
Ladybird, Ladybird
Andersen
1988 £5.95 24pp
0 86264 200 0

Despite its dramatic and tragic opening 'Ladybird, Ladybird, fly away home, Your house is on fire, your children are gone' this is a gentle book made calm by Ruth Brown's detailed, closely observed pictures. Based on the traditional nursery rhyme it tells the story of the ladybird trying to find her way home over cornfields and over trees, past a frog, a snail, a cat, a crow and a squirrel until a bee leads the way back to the nest where the children are still safe and waiting. Each picture is worth studying for its delicate, beautifully drawn and richly coloured painting.

11
BUTLER, Dorothy
My Brown Bear Barney
illustrated by Elizabeth
Fuller
Hodder & Stoughton
1989 £5.95 32pp
0 340 492567 0

When shopping, visiting, playing, gardening or getting ready for bed the little girl takes Brown Bear Barney with her. But what about when she goes to school? Mum says that bears don't go to school but the little girl has her own views. This is a simple story, told and illustrated with vigour.

12
COLE, Babette
King Change-a-lot
Hamish Hamilton
1988 £6.95 24pp
0 241 12491 3

In this latest of a series of 'royal' picture books (*Prince Cinders* and *Princess Smartypants*), the baby Prince Change-a-lot rises up in revolt against his misruling parents and ghastly nanny Miss Grumpbladder. With the help of the genie of the potty, Change-a-lot deposes his parents, reducing them to royal babies; turns the government office into a gigantic funfair; builds a rubber disco for the discontented giants; locks up all the bad fairies; and lives to be a very clever and popular king. The colour and wit of Babette Cole's illustrations bring alive this delightfully dotty story.

13
COWCHER, Helen
Rainforest
Andre Deutsch
1988 £5.95 32pp
0 233 982 663

The age old way of life of the animals in the rainforest is threatened by the tree fellers who hack down the trees without a thought for the past or the future. Helen Cowcher's beautiful, bright, bold illustrations capture the animals in their secret and mysterious habitat and show their terror at the changes that are wrought around them. *Rainforest* poses important questions about how much damage man and technology should be allowed to do to the environment.

14
DOWNIE, Jill
Alphabet Puzzle
Andersen
1988 £6.95 32pp
0 86264 205 1

Alphabet Puzzle is satisfying on two counts. The delicate, soft-toned artwork showing an axe, a camel, an egg and so on invites a lingering look, while the clever use of cut-outs hiding what comes next adds an element of excitement to the traditional ABC.

15
EYLES, Heather
Well I Never!
illustrated by Tony Ross
Andersen
1988 £5.95 32pp
0 86264 203 5

Well I Never! is a perfect and delightful mixture of fear and fun. The little girl cannot get dressed because there is a witch in her bedroom where the tee shirt is and a vampire in the bathroom with her shorts. Socks and shoes are impossible, too, on account of the werewolf on the stairs and the ghost in the cupboard under the stairs. When Mum takes a look she finds that every word is true. But is it?

16
FOREMAN, Michael
The Angel and the
Wild Animal
Andersen
1988 £5.95 32pp
0 86264 207 8

Parents and children alike will recognise and be amused by Michael Foreman's lifelike, but kindly, account of how the Angel can be a Wild Animal and sometimes, most times, just a little boy. The extreme emotions of childhood are powerfully captured in Michael Foreman's violent illustrations of floods and earthquakes caused by the Wild Animal set against the peaceful and tender illustrations of the Angel.

17
FUGE, Charles
Bush Vark's First
Day Out
Macmillan
1988 £6.50 32pp
0 333 46280 7

Charles Fuge's innocent little Bush Vark sets off on his first day's outing from the burrow. The little Bush Vark has no idea that he is easy prey for the hauntingly ugly predators who live around him. The juxtaposition of the vulnerable and the powerful is perfectly illustrated in Charles Fuge's strong and evocative artwork.

18
GOODALL, John S.
Story of a Farm
Andre Deutsch
1989 £5.95 24pp
0 233 98295 7

The huge range of activities which take place on a farm and how they have changed through the centuries are shown in John Goodall's paintings. A half-page flap enables Goodall to show two activities - bringing in the cows and feeding the horses - across one double spread background. The flap also gives the reader the impression that they are moving through time as the past gradually gives way to the present against a background of subtly changing countryside.

19
GORDON, Margaret
Mousetale
Viking Kestrel
1988 £6.95 32pp
0 670 81803 8

Mirabelle Mouse and Clarence the Cat work together (as friends!) to try to unscramble the problem of Mirabelle's extraordinarily long tail. A long mouse tail is easily mistaken for all sorts of things - a strand of spaghetti, a shoe lace, knitting wool or a giant worm - the perfect tea-time treat for a hungry bird. Nothing can be done until Mr Spanner lifts his spell, but then Mirabelle seems like a very tempting treat for a hungry cat. Margaret Gordon's cat escapade is full of jolly details.

20
GOWAR, Mick
A Hard Day's Work
illustrated by Margaret
Chamberlain
Andre Deutsch
1989 £5.95 32pp
0 233 98251 9

Mick Gowar's text cheerily describes how a little girl innocently(!) passes the time when she has to be taken to her father's office for the day because Mum is ill. Margaret Chamberlain's illustrations tell a quite different story. There's havoc from the first moment with colouring and cutting out in all the wrong places and buttons being pressed when they oughtn't. In despair, a worn out Dad takes his daughter home. Luckily Mum is feeling better because Dad retires to bed. Combined, the text and pictures give both the adult reader and the child looker much to enjoy.

21
GRAHAM, Richard
Jack and the Monster
illustrated by Susan Varley
Andersen
1988 £5.95 32pp
0 86264 212 4

The monster who lives in Jack's house isn't fierce and has no teeth but it is very noisy, very messy, a bit smelly and not very clever. Richard Graham describes just how Jack feels about the monster in his house - including his gradual acceptance of him. Susan Varley's artwork wittily captures all the moods and treads a clever line between giving the secret away and providing enough information to be reassuring.

22
GRAY, Nigel
A Country Far Away
illustrated by Philippe Dupasquier
Andersen
1988 £5.95 32pp
0 86264 204 3

The contrasts and the similarities between two boys' lives are neatly shown in Philippe Dupasquier's appealing illustrations. 'Today was just an ordinary day. I stayed at home' means the same for two boys even though their homes are quite different. One is a spacious house on a housing estate, the other a round hut in a dusty African village. And so on, through the text. 'I did a lot of jobs to help my mum and dad' shows one boy hoovering and gardening and the other carrying water for the crops and milking a goat. The clever conception of this picture book enables children to understand its message easily and well.

23
GRAY, Nigel
A Balloon for Grandad
illustrated by Jane Ray
Orchard
1988 £6.25 32pp
1 85213 125 X

When Sam's balloon escapes out of the back door he is distraught until his father explains that the balloon is on its way to visit his Grandad Abdulla living alone on an island. After a rather slow and fussy start the balloon and the book take off with glorious pictures showing the snow-decorated mountains, the sparkling blue-green sea, the hot yellow sand of the desert and the long blue ribbon of the river over which the balloon passes before it reaches Grandad Abdulla sitting peacefully in the shade of his mango tree. Nigel Gray's lyrical descriptions of the exotic landscape are matched perfectly by the action-filled, softly coloured illustrations showing a bird's-eye or balloon's-eye view of the same.

24
GRETZ, Susanna
Roger Loses His Marbles
Bodley Head
1988 £5.50 32pp
0 370 31138 8

Roger's determination to find his missing yellow marbles and his refusal to cheer up until they are found are reminiscent of any obsessional child. In Susanna Gretz's pig family Aunt Lulu is coming to stay. Not only must Roger tidy up his room for her but he has also got to move out of it and sleep in the baby's room. The marbles remain lost and Roger remains grumpy throughout the festivities. But a quite different mood prevails when Aunt Lulu disturbs him - with the marbles - in the middle of the night. The accurate and detailed observation makes this both an amusing story and one which rings true.

25
HADITHI, Mwenye
Tricky Tortoise
illustrated by Adrienne Kennaway
Hodder & Stoughton
1988 £6.95 32pp
0 340 42530 X

The tortoise in this story is as wily as his ancestor, the hero of the tale of Hare and Tortoise. With the help of his identical brother, the tortoise plays a clever trick on the stupid elephant to pay him out for stepping on him three hundred and thirty-three times. The simple and pleasing variation on a well-known fable is richly illustrated with powerful jungle settings at night and by day.

26
HAWKINS, Colin
HAWKINS, Jacqui
Noah Built an Ark One Day
Methuen
1989 £5.95 24pp
0 416 09412 0

'Noah built an ark one day, He knew a flood was on the way.' So begins this visually and verbally witty version of the Noah story in which Noah looks as if he might wish he had never suggested taking the animals, given how badly they are behaving. Lots of dialogue in bubble speech and flaps that open to reveal all kinds of chaos make this especially suitable for children to read on their own.

27
HENDERSON, Kathy
The Babysitter
Andre Deutsch
1988 £5.95 32pp
0 233 98214 0

How four children get the better of the babysitter may not be very edifying but it is a not uncommon occurrence. Kathy Henderson's fluid verse and her bright and bold pictures reflect the busy and untidy side of family life.

28
HOLABIRD, Katharine
Alexander and the Dragon
illustrated by Helen Craig
Aurum
1988 £4.95 32pp
1 85406 008 2

Katharine Holabird strikes just the right note in this understanding and reassuring story about a little boy who is frightened of the dark until he makes friends with the dragon who lives under his bed. Helen Craig's illustrations match the mood exactly.

29
IMPEY, Rose
A Letter to Father Christmas
illustrated by Sue Porter
Orchard
1988 £5.95 32pp
0 85213 126 8

Rose Impey's story is carefully and satisfyingly constructed without any sense of contrivance. It is magical but it also has the ring of absolute truth about it. Charlotte sends a surprising Christmas present list to Father Christmas by mistake, but the wrong list turns out to be right after all since it enables Charlotte to take care of the animals she is worried about.

30
JONAS, Ann
Reflections
Julia MacRae
1988 £5.95 32pp
0 86203 343 8

Ann Jonas's illustrations deceive the eye so that they can be looked at from right way up and from upside down giving two apparently different images from the same picture. The story takes a child getting up early to watch the dawn, the fishermen, the first ferry arriving, the boatyard, the mill and finally going into the scary wood where there are sometimes deer, before turning round (the cue for the reader to turn the book round) and going back through the same scenery but seeing quite different things. The pictures are beautiful in their own right. Their double interpretation is brilliant.

31
JONG, Eveline de
Isn't She Clever!
illustrated by Charlotte Firmin
Andre Deutsch
1988 £5.95 32pp
0 233 98261 2

By juxtaposing professionals of various kinds - gardener, cook, decorator - with Mum doing those jobs as part of her everyday life, Eveline de Jong, without the need for explanation, shows the important job which women at home are doing. Charlotte Firmin's illustrations are similarly understated.

32
KELLER, Holly
Geraldine's Big Snow
Julia MacRae
1988 £5.25 24pp
0 86203 363 2

Everyone is getting ready for the big snow that is forecast. Geraldine cannot wait. She's got her sledge down from the attic and her new boots are ready by the door. But the snow doesn't come. Geraldine goes outside to wait, in case that makes it come faster. By bedtime there is still no snow. Was the forecast wrong? Geraldine wakes up to a white world. She goes right up to the top of the highest hill and sledges down. Holly Keller captures a child's impatience, anticipation and delight.

33
KITAMURA, Satoshi
UFO Diary
Andersen
1989 £5.95 32pp
0 86264 209 4

'On Monday, I took a wrong turn in the Milky Way.' Satoshi Kitamura's spaceship travels through a lonely and texturally rich night sky before arriving at our own 'strange blue planet, bright as a glass ball'. Once landed, the alien and his earthling friend take a look at our planet from some new angles. *UFO Diary* is a book of enormous calm which encourages careful looking at the illustrations.

34
LIONNI, Leo
Six Crows
Andersen
1989 £6.95 32pp
0 86264 211 6

Through this simple fable Leo Lionni makes a stand against selfishness and encourages children to understand how much better co-operation is than confrontation. The six crows and the farmer reach a stalemate in their battle for control over the wheat crop. Only the intervention of the wise owl makes everything turn out all right. Leo Lionni's bright and dramatic collage gives the story vivid life.

35
McKEE, David
Who's a Clever Baby then?
Andersen
1988 £5.95 32pp
0 86264 201 9

Grandma tries and *tries* to get baby to talk, showing him all sorts of interesting things to name - a tiger, a bird, a fish, a crocodile - but baby has just one word, 'dog'. Or does he? David McKee's baby wins hands down in this excellent, funny, child-centred joke against all pushy adults.

36
McNAUGHTON, Colin
Jolly Roger and the
Pirates of Abdul the
Skinhead
Walker
1988 £8.95 40pp
0 7445 1011 2

Colin McNaughton's wholly integrated text and pictures are full of diabolical piratical jokes. They also tell a wonderfully ridiculous story of young Roger who is kidnapped by 'a pack of horrible, dirty, smelly, ugly, hairy, scary men' who stuff him into a sack and take him aboard the *Golden Behind*. From then on it's one adventure hot on the heels of another with the most audacious verbal play thrown in on the way.

37
MARTYR, Andrew
LAWFORD, Paula
Beeswax the Bad
Hamish Hamilton
1988 £6.95 32pp
0 241 12169 8

Beeswax is, without doubt, a really bad cat. His pranks get really out of hand but, when one of them backfires and Beeswax himself is hurt it is impossible not to feel sorry for him. The domestic chaos caused by this cat who would fit in well with T. S. Eliot's *Practical Cats* is vibrantly illustrated.

38
NARAHASHI, Keiko
I Have a Friend
A. & C. Black
1988 £5.95 40pp
0 7136 3061 2

'I have a friend who lives in my house.' A small boy plays with his shadow. They play in the park where the shadow can hide in the trees, they swim together with the shadow lurking darkly under the cool water. Sometimes the shadow goes to places where the boy cannot follow and then, at night, the shadow disappears. Keiko Narahashi's illustrations are quiet and still. They capture the strange, slightly magical relationship each of us has with our shadow.

39
PIENKOWSKI, Jan
Easter
Heinemann
1989 £6.95 32pp
0 434 95659 7

In the text of this book the Easter story is told through the words of the King James Version of the Bible. Jan Pienkowski's delicate, ornate and atmospheric silhouettes match the rich language of the Bible while also making it easily available to children.

40
PROVENSEN, Alice
PROVENSEN, Martin
Shaker Lane
Julia MacRae
1988 £6.95 32pp
0 86203 345 4

The cool, unhurried atmosphere of the beginning of *Shaker Lane* tempts readers to look closely at the countryside that is to provide the backdrop for every spread in the book. Taking that long look makes it possible to understand the profound changes which sweep over the countryside as people and their habits change. The Herkimer sisters live alone in a house facing the road, surrounded by scrubby, unkempt farmland. In order to live they sell off bits of their farm cheaply. Gradually, through the book, the empty fields become crowded with houses and children and dogs. They take up all the space; the countryside is blotted out. Then the wheel turns full circle. A reservoir is planned for the area. All the new houses will be flooded. Only the Herkimer sisters remain in their large house, high on the hill. The painterly illustrations to *Shaker Lane* make it a book to savour and enjoy.

41
ROCKWELL, Anne
Hugo at the Window
Hodder & Stoughton
1989 £6.95 32pp
0 340 43126 1

Hugo at the Window is a picture book which demands careful looking. Hugo the dog is left by his owner who is off on a mysterious mission. Hugo watches sadly from the window, not knowing why he has been left for so long. The reader, however, can follow the owner as he goes from shop to shop in the busy high street buying all kinds of things for Hugo.

42
ROSS, Tony
Super Dooper Jezebel
Andersen
1988 £5.95 32pp
0 86264 221 3

Jezebel's abrupt, unexpected and absolute comeuppance for being 'super dooper' makes *Super Dooper Jezebel* a brilliant book. Tony Ross goes to town with his visions of Jezebel as the perfect - and wholly objectionable - little girl. His and the reader's delight when her goodness leads to her downfall also needs, and gets, no apology. It is exactly right.

43
ROSS, Tony
I Want a Cat
Andersen
1989 £5.95 32pp
0 86264 237 X

Jessy wants a cat and is determined to have one. The pressure she puts on her parents quite quickly becomes irresistible. Any child who has ever tried to get the pet she wants will be delighted by Jessy's simple, foolproof method of achieving her goal.

44
SAMUELS, Vyanne
Carry Go Bring Come
illustrated by Jennifer
Northway
Bodley Head
1988 £5.95 32pp
0 370 31092 6

In all the bustle of a big wedding day Leon becomes more and more bedecked with shoes, gloves, head-dress and a pink flower as he runs up and down stairs fetching and carrying. 'Help,' he calls from the middle of the stairway when he can carry no more. Relieved of his load he hops back into bed gratefully. Vyanne Samuels' text begins with a distinct rhythm and sense of poem which is not fully sustained but the storyline is an amusing one and the pictures are exuberant and celebratory.

45
SIMMONDS, Posy
Lulu and the Flying
Babies
Cape
1988 £5.95 32pp
0 224 02526 0

No adult or child will feel quite the same about going to a museum after reading *Lulu and the Flying Babies*. Cross Lulu makes such a fuss in the museum that her dad leaves her

...and we spat out the stones down a mountain side....

on the bench until she cheers up. But Lulu is swiftly rescued by unexpected new friends who pop out of the pictures and take her on a series of delightful romps through the other canvases. There's snow to roll in, sea to splash in, a tiger to growl at and even cherries, apples and plums to eat. And then it's time to find Dad. Posy Simmonds' tenderness at its most entrancing is shown in the last picture of all - the elderly custodian helping two cheery little cherubs back into their picture.

46
STEADMAN, Ralph
No Room To Swing
A Cat
Andersen
1989 £5.95 32pp
0 86264 241 8

Ralph Steadman's exuberant cartoons make expansive play on a simple, well-constructed joke. Tom's room is too small to swing a cat, he complains. His mother makes various suggestions about how big it might be - big enough to swing a dog, a moose, an angry lion? Nope. All Tom wants is a room big enough to swing himself, a problem which is simply resolved by a trip to the park.

47
STEVENSON, James
No Need for Monty
Gollancz
1988 £6.95 32pp
0 575 04295 8

It's children against adults in *No Need for Monty* and in this case it is the children who win. Riding to school across the river on Monty's back has always suited the children just fine. But the adults are sure that there is a better and safer way. Each and every one of their various suggestions is ingenious but disastrous - the skyride snaps, the hot air balloon floats off with a mind of its own, the stilts get tangled up and everyone ends up soaking wet. In the end lovable, reliable Monty proves that he is the only sure and safe way for the kids to reach school. James Stevenson's picture books are always affectionate and funny.

48
SUNDGAARD, Arnold
The Lamb and the Butterfly
illustrated by Eric Carle
Hodder & Stoughton
1989 £6.95 32pp
0 340 49580 4

'Where is your home?' the Lamb asked the Butterfly. 'The world is my home,' answered the Butterfly. 'I am free to fly anywhere.' The contrast between the carefree but dangerous life of a butterfly and the tame but secure one of a lamb makes an excellent moral tale. Both the text with its fluttering for the butterfly and language for the lamb and the collage illustrations reflect the story perfectly.

49
VINCENT, Gabrielle
Get Better, Ernest!
Julia MacRae
1988 £5.95 24pp
0 86203 354 3

The little mouse Celestine tries to look after the big bear Ernest when he is sick. The doctor says he must stay in bed and eat a bland diet and drink tea. But bed is boring and Ernest wants a big meal and some coffee. Celestine is kept busy but she manages to nurse him and to keep him from being bored. Gabrielle Vincent's newest story about these two charming and vivacious characters has all the warmth of its predecessors.

50
VOAKE, Charlotte
Mrs Goose's Baby
Walker
1988 £5.95 24pp
0 7445 1138 0

Mrs Goose finds an egg and hatches it. She loves her new baby so much that she never notices that there is something very unusual about it. Child readers will enjoy knowing the joke that Mrs Goose cannot see in this effective combination of silliness and tenderness.

51
WADDELL, Martin
Can't You Sleep, Little Bear?
illustrated by Barbara Firth
Walker
1988 £6.95 32pp
0 7445 0796 0

It's bedtime and Little Bear cannot get to sleep. 'Can't you sleep, Little Bear?' asks Big Bear solicitously - even though it means dragging himself away from the book he is enjoying. Little Bear is scared. He wants a light, not a little lantern, not even a bigger lantern but a great big light. The biggest light that there is - the moon. Barbara Firth's illustrations set the story deep in a warm and cosy cave making *Can't You Sleep, Little Bear?* a perfect bedtime book.

52
WADDELL, Martin
The Park in the Dark
illustrated by Barbara
Firth
Walker
1989 £6.95 32pp
0 7445 0716 2

'When the sun goes down and the moon comes up and the old swing creaks in the dark, that's when we go to the park, me and Loopy and Little Gee, all three.' Martin Waddell's poetic text tells of how three soft toys steal out at the dead of night to play in the park. But the park at night is a frightening place, full of unexpected terrors. Barbara Firth's luminous night pictures capture the spirit and mood of the adventure absolutely.

53
WATTS, Bernadette
Tattercoats
North-South
1989 £6.95 32pp
1 55858 002 6

A gentle, sentimental story, *Tattercoats* tells of a scarecrow who misses the children who played with him in the summertime. The animals and birds bring him news of the children but Tattercoats must stay out in the fields in all weathers, rooted to the spot by his one leg. Finally he falls over completely and is rescued by the farmer and brought into the garden where he can see what is going on all the time. Bernadette Watts' text is a little soppy but her illustrations are nicely tender.

54
WELLINGTON, Monica
All My Little Ducklings
Aurum
1989 £5.95 32pp
1 85406 022 8

A day in the life of a family of bright, bold yellow ducklings, told mostly through the noises that they make as they go about their daily business. 'All my little ducklings waddle to the water, Scurry Hurry Plunk.' The attractive, primary colours and simple line of the artwork fit excellently with the spare text.

55
WILDSMITH, Brian
Carousel
Oxford
1989 £5.95 32pp
0 19 279853 7

Brian Wildsmith weaves a story of hope and magic through his jumble of bright, vivid illustrations. Rosie lies sick, too ill to move from her bed, too ill to get better. Her friends bring her pictures of her favourite carousel and in her dreams she hears 'Step aboard and we will fly, through the window, through the sky.' Rosie embarks on a fantastical ride which restores her hope and makes her well.

56
WILLIS, Jeanne
Dr Xargle's Book of
Earthlets
illustrated by Tony Ross
Andersen
1988 £5.95 32pp
0 86264 213 2

How we may seem to Aliens. Dr Xargle gives a lesson about Earthlets. There follow a series of hilarious pictures with apt texts. 'Earthlets have no fangs at birth. For many days they drink only milk through a hole in their face.' The eager Aliens learn much about their subjects. Then, donning suitable disguises, they set off for a closer inspection. Watch out babies everywhere!

57
WORTHINGTON,
Phoebe
Teddy Bear Boatman
Viking Kestrel
1988 £6.50 24pp
0 670 82171 3

The sixth in the delightful, determinedly dated stories about the little Teddy Bear who started out as a Coalman. Here he is a Boatman - 'He had a boat, a horse called Daisy, and a little sister called Suzy'. Teddy Bear Boatman and Suzy live on a beautifully painted barge which is pulled along by Daisy. Life on the canal slips by with details such as pushing the boat through a tunnel with their paws, delivering some hay and some coal and going through a lock. The text is plain and spare, the details come from the pretty and delicate illustrations.

58
ZATON, Jesus
The Night the Animals
Fought
illustrated by Jesus
Gabon
Mantra
1988 £5.95 32pp
0 947679 871

In a land parched by drought the animals
fight a vicious battle over the shiny round
object floating in the remaining pool. The
battle lasts all night until the squirrel suggests that everyone should share the shiny
ball. The tired animals agree but, when they
return to the pond as the sun comes up they
find the ball has disappeared. This pleasing
story of the night is beautifully illustrated by
Jesus Gabon's vivid pictures of all the animals
against a stark, drought-stricken background.

BEGINNING TO READ

The first stages of reading pass quickly for some children but are slow and sometimes painful for others. These books with a simple storyline and small vocabulary will help all beginning readers take steps towards independent reading.

59
GILLHAM, Bill
My Mum's a Window
Cleaner
illustrated by Margaret
Chamberlain
Methuen
1988 £2.95 32pp
0 416 09732 4

Lots of action and a refreshingly unlikely subject for new readers make *My Mum's a Window Cleaner* a stimulating book to learn from. Mum becomes a heroine when she rescues 'a baby with its bottle, a fat man having a bath and even an old lady with a parrot' from a burning house. And she likes doing it so much that she becomes a firelady instead. Based on the idea of paired reading this has a fairly complicated vocabulary which child and adult will be able to read and enjoy together.

60
HAYES, Sarah
This is the Bear and the
Picnic Lunch
illustrated by Helen Craig
Walker
1988 £3.95 32pp
0 7445 0555 0

'This is the boy who packed a lunch of sandwiches, crisps and an apple to crunch.' So begins Sarah Hayes's rhythmic, rhyming and tempting-to-read text. The text and Helen Craig's pictures together tell the story of how the guard teddy bear fails in his duty and allows the dog to raid the picnic. Bear, boy and dog end up cheerfully eating the picnic indoors. Simple bubbles of speech combined with the carefully chosen vocabulary of the main text, fully and wittily illustrated by the pictures, make this an ideal book for first readers.

61
VAN LEEUWEN, Jean
Amanda Pig and her Big
Brother Oliver
illustrated by Ann
Schweninger
Heinemann
1988 £5.95 56pp
0 434 94713 6

Each of these short stories captures accurately, sympathetically and from a child's viewpoint an episode in the lives of two siblings - little pigs, in this case. In 'The Best Trick' Amanda always wants to do whatever Oliver does. But, whether it is running, throwing or jumping all Amanda is able to do is fall over. Never mind, says Father, Amanda is the best at falling over. In 'Me Too' Oliver finds Amanda's copying nothing but a nuisance until Father suggests that he helps her be big like him. The simple and clearly printed text is matched by finely observed, very domestic illustrations.

62
WILKINS, Verna Allette
Mike and Lottie
illustrated by Alan Baker
Tamarind
1988 £4.95 32pp
1 870516 03 6

After a visit to the zoo Mike really wants an ocelot (the only unfamiliar word in the book). His dad says no to an ocelot but on Mike's birthday he gets a small cat, one that he can love and play with. Mike's story is freshly told in a simple, well laid out vocabulary. Alan Baker's quasi-photographic illustrations are both beautiful and arresting.

63
WILMER, Diane
Cat Nap
illustrated by Alan Snow
Octopus
1989 99p 30pp
1 85270 120 X

Cat Nap is an extremely simple text relating the Cat's search for a quiet place to sleep. The illustrations are bold and accurate, thus reinforcing the text. The use of speech bubbles makes the vocabulary especially approachable.

64
ZIEFERT, Harriet
Nicky Upstairs and
Down
illustrated by Richard
Brown
Puffin
1988 £2.50 32pp
0 14 032583 2 P

Within this likeable story there is a carefully controlled vocabulary based on the concept of up and down. The little kitten Nicky plays upstairs and downstairs, searches for his mother upstairs and downstairs and ends up waiting for her neither up nor down but right in the middle of the staircase. This is enough of both a picture book and a story book to make reading it worthwhile.

EARLY READING

Reading entirely alone without an adult listening, is a big step to take. It requires sufficient reading ability to get enough words right to keep the story alive. Exciting, funny, sad, imaginative - stories of all kinds are needed to enthrall their audience.

65
AHLBERG, Allan
Mrs Jolly's Joke Shop
illustrated by Colin
McNaughton
Viking Kestrel
1988 £3.95 24pp
0 670 81693 0
Puffin
1988 £1.95 24pp
0 14 032347 3 P

The success of *Mrs Jolly's Joke Shop* lies in the expert play which Allan Ahlberg makes on children's own love of jokes, combined with Colin McNaughton's witty visual interpretation of them. The story of the happenings in the joke shop is interspersed with favourite, familiar jokes - 'What's white on the outside, green on the inside and hops?' 'A frog sandwich!' and the like. Knowing these words already will help give confidence to tackle the rest, especially as the story itself is action-packed and funny too.

66
BOND, Ruskin
Ghost Trouble
illustrated by Barbara
Walker
Julia MacRae
1989 £3.50 48pp
0 86203 380 2

The Pret, a tiny invisible ghost that lives in the peepal tree, is forever playing tricks on passing tongas and bicycles. But things get worse when the Public Works Department decides to chop down the peepal tree forcing

the Pret to move into the house. Then everyone is at his mercy. He tweaks the parrot's feathers, and pulls off Uncle Benji's blankets at night. He hides granny's glasses and mixes up the toothpaste and the shaving cream. Moving seems to be the only answer but when the family try to move, the Pret makes it quite clear that he will do anything to stop them. This light-hearted ghosting is fun to read.

67
BYARS, Betsy
The Golly Sisters
Go West
illustrated by Sue
Truesdell
Gollancz
1989 £5.95 60pp
0 575 04468 3

May-May and Rose, the Golly sisters, are trying to set off for the West in their covered wagon but they can't even make the horse start. Is there a horse-word for start? At last the two sisters remember it but even when they are on their way all does not go smoothly. Betsy Byars' characters and storyline are original and funny, and her use of language is perfectly suited to give readers confidence. The combination, enhanced by witty and vigorous illustrations, makes *The Golly Sisters Go West* an excellent book for those just reading to themselves.

68
CAMERON, Ann
Julian's Glorious
Summer
illustrated by Ann
Strugnell
Gollancz
1989 £5.95 62pp
0 575 04117 X

Julian is looking forward to a long summer holiday playing with his best friend Gloria. But everthing is spoiled when Gloria appears on a beautiful, brand new bike. Consumed with jealousy Julian pretends not to care. Hasn't he always hated bikes? His parents allow him to wallow in his self pity for a while and then they come up with a solution which makes it a really glorious summer for Julian too. The story is wittily observed and written and Ann Strugnell's illustrations make it visually rich as well.

69
CRESSWELL, Helen
Two Hoots
illustrated by Colin West
A. & C. Black
1988 £3.95 62pp
0 7136 2982 7
Fontana
1988 £1.50 62pp
0 00 673006 X P

The totally integrated text and artwork of *Two Hoots* tells a delightfully dotty story about Big Owl and Little Owl who, far from being wise as owls are meant to be, are as daft as two coots. The other owls try to expel them from the woods, but the chance passing of a class outing puts paid to that and turns Big and Little Owl into heroes instead.

70
DUNBAR, Joyce
Mouse Mad Madeline
illustrated by James
Dunbar
Hamish Hamilton
1988 £3.95 32pp
0 241 12223 6

A simple wish turns Madeline into a mouse. Not that she minds and her parents seem not to notice though they are surprised that her clothes no longer fit and that she changes her eating habits rather dramatically. Only Grandma notices because she suggested the wish in the first place. Luckily all is made well, after a near mishap, and Madeline is happy to be a little girl again. A pleasing, well-controlled domestic and magic story.

71
FINE, Anne
Stranger Danger?
illustrated by Jean Baylis
Hamish Hamilton
1989 £2.75 42pp
0 241 12545 6

In this story Anne Fine looks at the confusion which can arise if children are made too suspicious of strangers. She draws careful and important distinctions between taking risks and being normally friendly or accepting innocuous help. The policeman makes such a meal of not going with strangers that Joe loses the ability to think for himself. He almost won't go with the eye-test lady even though she has his name on a list and at first he won't accept a peppermint from a strange man at the concert even though he is coughing so much that he is spoiling it for everyone else. It is better to be safe than sorry, but *Stranger Danger?* also shows that children must not be so frightened that they can no longer make sensible judgements of their own.

72
HARDCASTLE, Michael
The Magic Party
illustrated by Vanessa
Julian-Ottie
Blackie
1988 £2.95 48pp
0 216 92108 2

Two birthday parties on the same day and the same guests invited to each makes for problems. How will Katie's and Melanie's friends choose which party to go to? Melanie's sounds tempting because she is going to have a magician to entertain her guests but Katie's mum comes up with a magic idea which makes both parties more successful.

73
HENDRY, Diana
The Not-Anywhere
House
illustrated by Mei-Yim
Low
Julia MacRae
1989 £3.50 48pp
0 86203 352 7

Like many children faced with moving, Hannah is unhappy at the thought of leaving her old home for a new, unknown one. Her parents do everything possible to cheer her up beforehand but it is not until she finds the special tree right outside her window that Hannah realises that she will be happy in the new home. Diana Hendry writes a familiar story with tenderness and gives it an optimistic feel.

74
IMPEY, Rose
KNOX, Jolyne
Desperate for a Dog
A. & C.Black
1988 £3.95 64pp
0 7136 2980 0
Fontana
1988 £1.50 64pp
0 00 673007 8 P

Desperate for a Dog is a story told in a perfect blend of straight narrative and amusing speech bubbles and pictures. The campaign to get a dog is launched. Mum wavers, but Dad is adamant and, since he is the one at home all day, it is his view that holds sway. Four rounds later - or four chapters later - the girls begin to look as if they might win. They are lent a dog to look after. From then on it is a short step to the final round and Dad's total defeat. With their witty, child-centred approach Rose Impey and Jolyne Knox have given fresh life to a tired storyline.

75
IMPEY, Rose
Scare Yourself to Sleep
illustrated by Moira
Kemp
Ragged Bears
1988 £4.95 46pp
1 870817 06 0

Two little girls are sleeping out for the night. They won't let a younger brother in - that would spoil everything. They amuse themselves by telling more and more frightening stories. There are the dustbin demons, the flying cat, the tree creeper and, most frightening of all, The Invisible Man. With Simon prowling about outside trying to get in, each one of these becomes horribly real. Rose Impey and Moira Kemp succeed in being extremely frightening but ultimately safe with an excellent resolution.

76
JOY, Margaret
The Little Explorer
illustrated by Toni Goffe
Viking Kestrel
1989 £3.99 95pp
0 670 82281 7

A zany adventure story, *The Little Explorer* is full of interesting surprises. Stanley is off to Allegria to search for the pinkafrillia, the rarest flower in the world. Knots the sailor and Peckish the parrot accompany him and together they make their way through the dangerous and unpredictable jungle.

77
LEESON, Robert
Never Kiss Frogs!
illustrated by David
Simonds
Hamish Hamilton
1988 £2.75 42pp
0 241 12489 1

Gail has a habit of kissing frogs, hoping that one of them will turn into a handsome prince and carry her and her mother off to live a life of luxury. But, when a frog does come to life, he turns out to be a far from perfect human. Robert Leeson's joke is quite sophisticated for this level but he tells it with wit and perception.

78
MOONEY, Bel
I Can't Find It!
illustrated by Margaret
Chamberlain
Methuen
1988 £5.95 48pp
0 416 13092 5

Children and parents will both enjoy these stories about Kitty who is forever losing things. Bel Mooney writes lightly and fluently and her eye for domestic detail is sharp. She makes quite serious points about losing courage and losing the way without ever preaching.

79
MORGAN, Alison
A Walk with Smudge
illustrated by Janet
Duchesne
Julia MacRae
1989 £3.50 48pp
0 86203 353 5

The simple storyline of *A Walk with Smudge* and the pace of the action make it both an easy and a satisfying book to read. Smudge runs away from Jeremy and leaps onto a bus. He seems to know where he wants to get off, too. Jeremy follows and finds that there is indeed a purpose behind Smudge's action.

80
PEARCE, Philippa
Freddy
illustrated by David
Armitage
Andre Deutsch
1988 £3.95 48pp
0 233 98175 6

Freddy is a domestic drama that is full of insight and understanding: insight into how parents behave and understanding of how children really feel. Sam cannot sleep without his beloved, threadbare rag - Freddy. When Mum goes away Sam needs Freddy straight away, but Freddy is nowhere to be found. Sam and Danny look everywhere. Dad looks - like a whirlwind - all round the house. No Freddy. The whole weekend is dominated by the absence of Freddy and by different attempts to find or replace him. (Dad's solution is by far the worst.) And then Mum comes home, with Freddy who has stowed away in her luggage. *Freddy* is a dramatic and wholly child-centred story.

81
PEYTON, K. M.
Plain Jack
illustrated by K. M.
Peyton
Hamish Hamilton
1988 £3.95 32pp
0 241 12146 9

A thoroughly horsy, moral tale, *Plain Jack* tells of the lives of two foals born at the same time but to different fates. Fire of England is spoiled by his mother who tells him how many races he will win and how clever he is. Plain Jack is born to a plain mum who makes sure he knows that winning comes from hard work and good behaviour. Good, hard working Jack does his best and does well while Fire of England goes to the bad, redeemed only by Jack and the kind stable boy, Barney. K. M. Peyton's horse's-eye view convinces absolutely.

82
POWLING, Chris
Bella's Dragon
illustrated by Robert
Bartelt
Blackie
1988 £2.95 48pp
0 216 92403 0

The dragon that suddenly plops down in Bella's back garden is desperately looking for a new den - a nice, warm, cosy place to live. The estate agent makes no useful suggestions and Bella and the dragon have little success when they try a garage, a swimming pool and a superstore. It is only when the school heating breaks down that two problems can be solved at once. Chris Powling's light touch makes this a dragon story with a difference.

83
PULLEIN-THOMPSON,
Christine
The Big Storm
illustrated by Lesley
Smith
Hodder & Stoughton
1988 £3.95 32pp
0 340 48868 9

The Big Storm combines a cosy, domestic story with dramatic incidents. The wind outside is so fierce that Annie and Martin are frightened to stay in their beds. Outside a huge tree has crashed to the ground. In a lull in the wind they hear a faint mewing. Martin rushes out and makes a daring rescue.

84
RYLANT, Cynthia
Henry and Mudge
illustrated by Sucie
Stevenson
Gollancz
1989 £5.95 40pp
0 575 04483 7

Henry has no brothers and no sisters and there are no other children in his street. Henry is desperate for a dog. At last his mum and dad agree and Henry chooses a dog for himself. He chooses Mudge. Cynthia Rylant's simple text tells the story of a boy and his dog exactly from a child's viewpoint.

85
STONBOROUGH,
Margaret
The Father Christmas
Trap
illustrated by Sarah
Lenton
A. & C. Black
1988 £3.95 64pp
0 7136 3058 2

Doubters and believers alike will enjoy *The Father Christmas Trap* while also being able to retain their own opinion about what *exactly* happens on the night before Christmas. Andrew, Christopher and Sarah settle down quietly on Christmas Eve. They know the rules about being asleep. But then the holly bursts the balloon and they are all wide awake. What if they set a trap for Father Christmas just so that they can see him once? Much work later the trap is laid, the lights are off, everyone is asleep and . . . The story is as carefully worked out as the trap and as funny, while the illustrations with their witty asides and bubble speech make the reading easy.

FLUENT READING

Fluent readers have the skill to delight in reading. In books they can find new worlds to explore, new opinions to consider, new attitudes to adopt and a new language to take as their own. In subject matter and levels of sophistication there is an enormous range of choice among the following titles.

86
AIKEN, Joan
The Erl King's Daughter
illustrated by Paul Warren
Heinemann
1988 £2.50 48pp
0 434 93054 7

The Erl King's Daughter is a strong and sinister story. Kev is very much alone and easily frightened when the new girl Nora arrives at the school. He knows all. about the Erl King, who rides around at night on a black horse that is as fast as the wind but quiet, from the stories his gran has told him. When Nora tells him that she is the Erl King's daughter he believes her, and is horribly under her power until he remembers what his gran said about people from the dark and letting them go. As his own confidence is rebuilt the power of the Erl King's daughter is destroyed.

87
ALCOCK, Vivien
The Thing in the Woods
illustrated by Sally Holmes
Hamish Hamilton
1989 £3.50 81pp
0 241 12544 8

Jenny and Bill meet the strange 'thing' when they are out in the woods walking the dog. Of course no one believes them but it is true and the 'thing' is real enough, and friendly. Vivien Alcock's story is a comfortable mixture of fear and affection.

88
ASHLEY, Bernard
Down-And-Out
illustrated by Jane Cope
Orchard
1988 £3.95 64pp
1 85213 077 6

Bernard Ashley's perceptive story is told simply and tenderly but without over-sentimentality. He describes how a lonely old lady's life is changed by the sudden arrival of a young down-and-out from the local hostel. Nellie Powell has lived on her own in Clipper Street since her husband's death. Normally suspicious of strangers she finds in herself a soft spot for this nicely spoken, well-mannered young man. They spend a happy day together and Nellie looks optimistically forward to the next day. But William doesn't return. *Down-And-Out* is a thought-provoking book about the different ways we judge people we don't know.

89
BARRY, Margaret Stuart
The Witch and the
Holiday Club
illustrated by Linda
Birch
Collins
1988 £4.95 96pp
0 00 184922 0

Margaret Stuart Barry's witch has been developing her personality throughout the course of several books. She and her friend Simon now reappear in a new collection of stories about how they fill the long, hot hours of the summer holiday. As usual the witch's schemes become increasingly wild and hilarious. With Simon as an anchor and the witch up to her tricks, there is a great deal of dotty and amusing adventure.

90
BAWDEN, Nina
Keeping Henry
illustrated by Ian
Newsham
Gollancz
1988 £7.95 93pp
0 575 04256 7

Keeping Henry is a charming story which makes its points subtly. Set in the war it is the dramatic account of how three children and their mother, living in the country as evacuees, adopt and keep a squirrel in their house. Henry becomes an important member of the family, offering a centre for affection at a time of displacement and uncertainty. His eventual, unintentional return to his own habitat causes huge sadness to the narrator, while she also shows just how easily her younger brother accepts the loss as part of the war which brings so many changes.

91
BLACKER, Terence
Ms Wiz Spells Trouble
illustrated by Toni Goffe
Piccadilly
1988 £5.25 52pp
1 85340 022 X

The sparkling, zany humour of *Ms Wiz Spells Trouble* lights up this story from the very beginning. Ms Wiz is the new teacher for the notoriously difficult Class Three. Is she a witch? Is she a hippy? Is she good or is she bad? No one knows for sure. Terence Blacker's skilful writing of this familiar story has resulted in a brilliantly funny book.

92
CATE, Dick
Foxcover
illustrated by Caroline
Binch
Gollancz
1988 £7.95 160pp
0 575 04292 3

Dick Cate's characters, their interaction with each other and, especially, their dialogue are all refreshingly lifelike. The jokes that they make are children's jokes; their observations, similarly, have a proper child-like perspective. *Foxcover* has drama. Billy's expulsion from the gang, his emergence as an independent and developing character, and his final reversed role situation with Butch keep the story going, but the strength of the book lies in Dick Cate's real understanding of his setting - a small community facing strikes and the resulting violence - and how the children of that community speak and play.

93
COLE, Hannah
Kick-Off
illustrated by Iain
McCraig
Julia MacRae
1989 £3.50 48pp
0 86203 340 3

Kick-Off is a book about girls playing football with convincing characters and a strong setting even though the story itself is fairly predictable. Football-mad Paula and Shazia persuade the teacher to let them try for the school team - and get chosen. In the match they prove how well they can play, thus squashing the prejudice from the boys. All familiar ground, but Hannah Cole's story stands out for the credibility of its relationships between the boys and the girls and the domestic background of both Paula and Shazia.

94
CORBALIS, Judy
Oskar and the Ice-Pick
illustrated by David
Parkins
Andre Deutsch
1988 £6.50 176pp
0 233 98181 0

Oskar and the Ice-Pick starts at a great pace. Oskar's mother is a famous mountaineer. His granny, who insists on being called Elspeth, is a famous swimmer. Both are really too busy to look after Oskar. It looks as if Oskar will be left behind while they go off and be famous until Henrietta the Gorillagram arrives with a message 'PLEASE BRING ICEPICK URGENTLY'. Oskar and Henrietta fly off to the Himalayas with the ice-pick where they fail to find Oskar's mother but have some incredible adventures with Khones and ice creams of all different kinds. The plot and action wear a little thin before the end but the humour endures.

95
CREBIN, June
Ride to the Rescue
illustrated by Catherine
Bradbury
Viking Kestrel
1989 £4.50 96pp
0 670 82424 0

The main plot of *Ride to the Rescue* is a familiar girl-longs-for-a-pony story but June Crebin has set it in an exciting and credible adventure and peopled it with convincing characters. When Kate's father promises her that she will soon have a pony of her own she thinks he means for life, not just for a holiday. But through having Blanco for the holiday, and with the help of her new half brother, she finds a way of getting a pony of her own forever.

96
CROSSLEY-HOLLAND,
Kevin
Piper and Pooka
illustrated by Peter
Melnyczuk
Orchard
1988 £3.95 64pp
1 85213 093 8

Piper and Pooka is the title story of these four brief stories of boggarts, bogles and other strange creatures. In it Patsy the piper meets a strange creature who leads him on an unlikely night-time trail which ends in riches and new skills. Or does it? In 'the Farmer and Boggart' Terry buys a new farm but finds part of it haunted by a boggart whom he must outwit three times before he can claim the land for his own. Kevin Crossley-Holland gives his stories a traditional flavour and vigour.

97
CURTIS, Philip
Mr Browser and the
Space Maggots
illustrated by Tony Ross
Andersen
1989 £5.95 126pp
0 86264 244 2

Mr Browser and the Space Maggots is an excellent combination of the everyday and the fantastic. Firmly based in a funny school setting with Mr Browser, the hard pressed, anxious and wholly sympathetic teacher, and Selwyn, Anna, Spiky and the rest of Class 8 as convincing children who converse in interesting and amusing dialogue, there is also a wild space fantasy about the space maggots which cause no end of trouble, especially for Mr Browser.

98
DEARY, Terry
The Dream Seller
illustrated by Alex Ayliffe
A. & C. Black
1988 £4.50 72pp
0 7136 3068 X

The Dream Seller has an excellent and refreshingly different storyline. The Dream Seller sends beautiful dreams to everyone in Duckpool but there's a catch, as soon becomes evident. The Dream Seller is a nasty, scheming blackmailer who, if not paid for good dreams, will send terrible, frightening, nightmarish ones instead. Tommy Trotter and his friend Alberta are determined to thwart him and many adventures later, they duly do. Duckpool and the characters in it are somewhat lifeless, but the central drama and the basic idea are quite absorbing enough.

99
FINE, Anne
Bill's New Frock
illustrated by Philippe
Dupasquier
Methuen
1988 £5.95 96pp
0 416 12152 7

Anne Fine's funny story makes sharp points about the sexist ways in which children are treated and, because it is seen through the eyes of a child, it makes them directly to children. Unaccountably, Billy wakes up one morning as a girl and is sent off to school in a beautiful pink dress. From then on, everything is different. He is not tripped up and sent flying by big Malcolm. Instead, and even worse, he is wolf-whistled! In the playground he discovers that there isn't much for the girls to do, given that the boys take up most of the space playing football. When he and Rohan brawl he finds that everyone blames Rohan. A *girl* wouldn't cause that kind of trouble - would she? *Bill's New Frock* will make readers laugh and think.

100
FLEISCHMAN, Sid
The Whipping Boy
illustrated by Tony Ross
Methuen
1988 £5.95 96pp
0 416 08812 0

Objectionable though the idea of a whipping boy is, Sid Fleischman has fashioned a ridiculous and rollicking, semi-historical story around one. Jemmy is the benighted whipping boy to a royal prince known universally as Prince Brat. Prince Brat is ignorant, lazy and conceited. Jemmy is quick-witted, well educated (he has done all the prince's learning for him) and basically quite kindly. When the prince runs away the whipping boy must go too - and just as well that he does since it is Jemmy who gets the two boys out of every possible trouble. Many adventures later, when the two finally return home, Prince Brat is a wiser and nicer boy - a satisfying resolution to a sharply funny story.

101
GERAS, Adele
The Fantora Family Files
illustrated by Tony Ross
Hamish Hamilton
1988 £6.95 106pp
0 241 12467 0

Narrated by an unusually intelligent cat, *The Fantora Family Files* is a zany family saga of a different kind. The difference is that the Fantoras are a far from usual family. Grandmother Filomena knits, as any grandmother might, but her knitting means all kinds of strange and unexpected things and the wool selects itself. Auntie Varvara has changed her name to the Eastern European spelling because she is determined to find the unlikely - a vegetarian vampire with a view to romance. The children, Bianca, Francesca and Marco have their own quirks mostly on account of the special powers they can use to good, bad or anyway unusual effect. Adele Geras' characters are normal enough to convince and eccentric enough to amuse.

102
GLEITZMAN, Morris
Two Weeks with the
Queen
Blackie
1989 £6.95 127pp
0 216 92761 7

Much of the storyline of *Two Weeks with the Queen* is completely over the top and yet the pace of the action and the emotional integrity of its theme make it a remarkably exciting, moving and funny book. When Colin's brother is suddenly ill on Christmas Day Colin thinks little of it. Given the quantity Luke ate it's not surprising that he'd end up in hospital with something gastric. But Luke is seriously ill with cancer and when Colin is told that he will die, he is determined to go to the top to get help. Sent to London to stay with well meaning but unhelpful relations, Colin puts all his energies into getting to the top - the Queen first and, failing her, the best cancer doctor in the world. Morris Gleitzman tells the story from Colin's point of view, exactly as Colin or readers of his story would see it.

103
HARRISON, Michael
Bags of Trouble
illustrated by David
McKee
Andersen
1988 £4.95 98pp
0 86264 219 1

The story of how Matthew gets involved in a series of mix-ups with bags, computers and teachers is light hearted, funny and convincing. Matthew's misapprehension about the computer tape which lists all the computers in the local schools is quite understandable. Michael Harrison understands how children react and the chain of events that follows one simple mistake is carefully and dramatically shaped.

104
HOFFMAN, Mary
Dracula's Daughter
illustrated by Chris
Riddell
Heinemann
1988 £2.50 42pp
0 434 93048 2

When Mr and Mrs Batty find a baby abandoned on their doorstep they immediately take her in and adopt her. She looks so sweet that they call her Angela. Angela grows up just like all good girls should until she starts growing her second teeth - funny, sharp, pointed things, not at all like other little girls. But the real trouble begins at Hallowe'en when Angela asks for a proper party and an uninvited, but not unexpected, guest appears. Mary Hoffman's Dracula story is cleverly constructed and told with an excellent balance of fear and fun.

105
JOY, Margaret
You're in the Juniors
Now
illustrated by Jo
Burroughes
Faber
1988 £6.95 132pp
0 571 15008 X

Margaret Joy gives an accurate view of the change that children perceive and experience when they move from Infants to Juniors. She catches the ups and downs of Foxy's class who start the year by wishing they were back with the cosy Mrs Griffiths but are quickly delighted by all the interesting things that Juniors do. Each of the twelve stories reflects a month in the exciting new year.

106
KAYE, Geraldine
Summer in Small Street
illustrated by Joanna
Carey
Methuen
1989 £5.95 65pp
0 416 13292 8

Geraldine Kaye uses the structure of a small terrace street with its identical houses but very different occupants as a framework for this collection of inter-related stories. Ben is newly arrived in the street but he soon makes friends with Charlene, Leroy, Tong, Sharon and Mrs Robinson, his new teacher. Each of the interwoven stories makes a gentle point which reflects the particular characters of the different children.

107
KING-SMITH, Dick
Martin's Mice
illustrated by Jez
Alborough
Gollancz
1988 £6.95 127pp
0 575 04264 8

Martin is a far from average kitten. His brothers call him a wimp and a wally because he thinks mice are sweet little things. He is a disgrace to his mum who makes him eat up his fresh mouse meat. But mouse meat makes Martin feel sick and he can't wait till he can leave home and fend for himself. Out on his own in the farmyard Martin is free. Unfortunately the mousing instinct is a strong one. Martin catches the first mouse he sees. The difference is that Martin keeps his mouse - as a pet. But one mouse soon becomes many mice and Martin is caught up in the complications of parenthood and a growing family. As usual Dick King-Smith gives a hilarious picture of farmyard life turned upside down.

108
LEESON, Robert
Hey Robin
illustrated by Helen
Leetham
A. & C. Black
1989 £4.50 64pp
0 7136 3120 1

Hey Robin is the deeply moral story of a young lad whose one wish in the world is that he might be brave and strong. The mysterious Old Meg promises to grant his wish on condition that he journeys to the Blue Mountains and collects a flask of clear spring water. The thing he must remember is that 'Happiness or pain/Is for you to choose/When you give you gain/When you take, you lose'. Robert Leeson tells his traditional tale as a modern parable.

109
LISHAK, Antony
Coming Round
illustrated by Heloise
Wire
A. & C. Black
1989 £4.50 54pp
0 7136 3119 8

Three distinct story-telling voices make *Coming Round* tense and vivid. There is what Colin is thinking but cannot say as he lies in a coma; there is the poem which drums in his brain telling him some of what really happened but hiding the truth until the very end; and there is the ordinary dialogue that goes on around him. Antony Lishak has shaped his story well so that the ending comes as a real surprise.

110
MacLACHLAN, Patricia
Seven Kisses in a Row
illustrated by Tudor
Humphries
Julia MacRae
1989 £3.50 48pp
0 86203 341 1

Emma is not looking forward to being minded by her uncle and aunt while her parents are away. At first she misses all the things that her parents do automatically but then she finds out how much she can teach Evelyn and Elliot and how much they can learn from her. *Seven Kisses in a Row* is a pleasing if sentimental story about a child teaching her aunt and uncle the subtleties of parenting.

111
MAHY, Margaret
The Blood and Thunder
Adventure on
Hurricane Peak
illustrated by Wendy
Smith
Dent
1989 £7.95 141pp
0 460 07031 2

Margaret Mahy's writing and ideas career along at a breathless pace. Her pastiche of a villainly adventure is far more exciting than most originals in the genre. *The Blood and Thunder Adventure on Hurricane Peak* starts with an unusual setting - the Unexpected School on top of Hurricane Peak which towers over the city of Hookywalker. The characters and the plot are every bit as unusual as the setting. The internal logic of the whole and the sheer inventiveness of everything about it make it a sparkling novel.

112
MORPURGO, Michael
My Friend Walter
Heinemann
1988 £7.95 156pp
0 434 95203 6

Michael Morpurgo brings history alive in this attractive adventure which revolves around the ghost of Sir Walter Raleigh. When ten-year-old Elizabeth Throckmorton visits the Tower of London she finds herself chatting to the model of Sir Walter Raleigh. But the model is alive and desperate to get back to Devon - Sir Walter's old home and Elizabeth's too. The ghost of Sir Walter travels back with Elizabeth and gets into all kinds of trouble - as only ghosts can - on her family's farm. The Throckmortons are having trouble keeping the farm and in the end it is Sir Walter, with his ridiculously bold plan, who saves Elizabeth's family while also restoring himself to his own home.

113
POWLING, Chris
Ziggy and the Ice Ogre
illustrated by Peter
Firmin
Heinemann
1988 £2.50 42pp
0 434 93051 2

Ziggy and the Ice Ogre is a zany story of refreshing originality. In Fountain City the fountains pour out a steady stream of different flavoured ice cream. Where does it all come from? Ziggy believes the stories about the Ice Ogre living under the ground and always remembers to thank him for his providence. But then the fountains dry up. The people of the city are starving until Ziggy tunnels down and sorts out the problems of both the Ice Ogre and the city.

114
SCOTT, Hugh
The Shaman's Stone
Andersen
1988 £5.95 110pp
0 86264 195 0

Spirits from times past convincingly haunt those of today who disturb their resting place in this terrifying story of unknown creatures and forces. Hugh Scott has crammed much, too much perhaps, into a short novel but the dramatic intensity of *The Shaman's Stone* and the quality of the descriptions make it a powerful novel.

115
SHEMIN, Margaretha
The Little Riders
illustrated by Peter Spier
Julia MacRae
1989 £6.95 80pp
0 86203 400 0

A view of how the occupation of Holland in the Second World War affected ordinary life in the towns and villages is given through the eyes of eleven-year-old Johanna. Johanna is staying with her grandparents when war breaks out. There is no way that she can be reunited with her parents in America until the war is over so she sees everything that goes on around her. For her, and for all the villagers, the twelve little riders who appear from the church on the chiming of every hour are the symbol of freedom. Everything must be done to keep them safe from the Germans who may at any moment want to melt them down for armaments. Johanna's part in the campaign gives real drama to a story that is full of mood and feeling.

116
SOUTTER, Andy
Scrapyard
illustrated by Satoshi Kitamura
A. & C. Black
1988 £4.50 72pp
0 7136 2998 3

Scrapyard is a novel of mysterious memories set against the harsh background of a pile of old scrap. Des steps off a train when he hears a faint noise from the scrapheap and finds himself trapped in a series of improbable adventures. Andy Soutter's story is tense and richly imaginative.

117
STANNARD, Russell
The Time of Space and Uncle Albert
illustrated by John Levers
Faber
1989 £6.99 128pp
0 571 15130 2

The point of Russell Stannard's story is to describe the extraordinary notion of Einstein's Theory of Relativity within a fictional framework. In that he is successful. His explanations are both lucid and readable. The surrounding, fast-moving story and Uncle Albert, an Einstein figure himself, are sometimes excessively puerile, but the juxtaposition means that readers who might be daunted by the Theory will be absorbed by the drama.

118
STRONG, Jeremy
Liar, Liar, Pants on Fire!
illustrated by Colin Paine
A. & C. Black
1988 £4.50 72pp
0 7136 2997 5

Jeremy Strong writes sensitively about how Susie handles moving from the town and her friends to a small village where she knows no one. The lies she tells seem to slip out, first to protect herself in her new environment and then to make her situation seem less miserable in a letter to her old friend. The gradual emergence of a stronger and happier Susie convinces.

119
TALBOT, John
Big Swig and Fling
illustrated by John Talbot
A. & C. Black
1988 £4.50 72pp
0 7136 2995 9

Big Swig the anteater and Fling the sneaky weasel are a couple of daring crooks. The only problem is that their daring is outreached by their incredible stupidity. John Talbot's variation on cops and robbers is funny and fast moving.

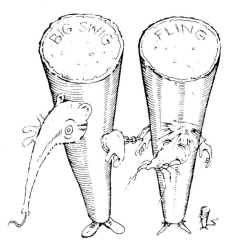

120
THOMAS, Ruth
The Class That
Went Wild
Hutchinson
1988 £6.50 226pp
0 09 173618 8

When their teacher is away Class 4L go completely wild. No other teacher seems able to control them at all. Gillian is worried about the fact that it is hard to learn anything in such a disruptive atmosphere but she is especially worried about her brother Joseph who is heading for real trouble. Ruth Thomas gets the feel of the individuals in the class and their interactions and leaves the drama to be resolved by the children in a most satisfactory way.

121
TOMLINSON, Theresa
The Water Cat
Julia MacRae
1988 £7.95 128pp
0 86203 367 5

The Water Cat is a complicated but absorbing blend of magic and folk history tightly woven together. Jane and Tom are newly arrived in a steel-working village in the 1950s. At night Jane is haunted by mysterious dreams and visions while in the daytime she and Tom with their friend Fred find a strange water cat - a shape-changing creature who leads them to unravel the episode of past history which is haunting Jane.

122
TOWNSON, Hazel
Fireworks Galore!
illustrated by Philippe
Dupasquier
Andersen
1988 £4.95 68pp
0 86264 214 0

Hazel Townson tells this adventure with enormous vigour and pace and with enough twists and turns to hold the reader's attention absolutely. Lenny borrows his dad's oldest trousers for the spectacular Guy Fawkes which he and his best mate Jake are making. But the jeans have something very valuable hidden in the pocket - Dad's special birthday present for Mum - and the jeans have gone missing. The chase for the missing jeans and their precious cargo is action packed and, happily, resolved.

123
URE, Jean
Soppy Birthday
illustrated by Beverley
Lees
Orchard
1988 £3.95 64pp
1 852 13 085 7

In a short, readable story Jean Ure tackles the straitjacket which peer pressure produces. Ben has always wanted a recorder but it would be a soppy thing to ask for for his birthday. His gang expects its members to be tough and disruptive, not interested in anything as conforming as music. Ben goes along with them doing everything he can to fit in and has the good luck to get his recorder into the bargain.

124
WADDELL, Martin
Tales From the Shop
That Never Shuts
illustrated by Maureen
Bradley
Viking Kestrel
1988 £5.95 96pp
0 670 82066 0

McGlone is an important person in End Cottages. She is the leader of McGlone's gang. Not a big gang, the only other members are Biddy, Buster and Flash, but a good gang nonetheless. Set in a tiny row of cottages by the shore, this is a collection of five stories about the children who live there and some of the things that happen to them. Through both his characters, whom he understands perfectly, and his setting, Martin Waddell evokes a strong and convincing sense of how things happen in a small community.

125
WALKER, Alice
To Hell With Dying
illustrated by Catherine
Deeter
Hodder & Stoughton
1988 £7.95 32pp
0 340 43022 2

Alice Walker's story of an old man's death is life affirming. Mr Sweet plays the guitar and lives on a neglected cotton farm. He is a diabetic and an alcoholic, and he has faced death and escaped on several occasions. *To Hell With Dying* is narrated by one of Mr Sweet's friends, a young girl growing up, whose life has been enchanted by Mr Sweet's strange talents and especial gift with children. Now she must face the fact that he can escape death no longer. Catherine Deeter's illustrations capture the exuberance and the pathos of this important story.

126
WESTALL, Robert
The Creature in the Dark
illustrated by Liz Roberts
Blackie
1988 £5.95 112pp
0 216 92427 8

Robert Westall makes tangible Sammy's fear of the mysterious beast which is savaging his father's sheep. One by one the lambs are disappearing without trace. Sammy is frightened of telling his father since he can offer no proof or explanation. When he does find out the reason he doesn't want his father to know for fear that the beast will be killed. The excitement of the story is made substantial by the convincing period farming background and characters.

127
WHYBROW, Ian
The Sniff Stories
illustrated by Toni Goffe
Bodley Head
1988 £5.95 128pp
0 370 31277 5

The predicaments of Ben Moore ring true. The description of his family - a baby sister, vague parents and an over-zealous aunt - and the accounts of how the dog Sniff first becomes a member of the family and then visits school are fun to read and perfectly plausible. Ian Whybrow's first person narrative has a pleasingly naive note.

Through hearing stories children begin to enjoy the tales told by others. They learn the delights of sharing a story and can understand the pleasures that come from reading to themselves.

128
BLISHEN, Edward
BLISHEN, Nancy
A Treasury of Stories for
Six Year Olds
illustrated by Tizzie
Knowles
Kingfisher
1988 £7.95 160pp
0 86272 330 2

The old-fashioned ring of a Treasury is belied by the fresh feel of this collection of stories - old and new - gathered from all over the world. There are vivid contemporary stories such as Philippa Pearce's 'Brainbox' about a horse without much brain (despite his name) who sets out in search of a companion horse, and Margaret Mahy's 'Don't Cut the Lawn' as well as the much anthologised, ever delightful 'The Wonderful Cake-Horse' by Terry Jones. Edward Blishen's own retelling of a Ugandan tale, 'Hare and Crocodile', which tells of how the crocodile is tricked out of his eggs by the greedy hare, adds a new story to an old tradition.

129
CARROLL, Lewis
Alice's Adventures in
Wonderland
illustrated by Anthony
Browne
Julia MacRae
1988 £12.95 128pp
0 86203 324 1

The story of Alice's extraordinary adventures in the strange Wonderland world is given fresh life through Anthony Browne's brilliant, interpretive illustrations. Alice herself is the beautiful little girl she should be. Anthony Browne shows her falling headlong down a strangely fascinating rabbit hole and then growing, shrinking, in the pool of tears, with the Gryphon and the Mock Turtle and much more. Each picture has twists and turns of its own, as well as capturing Lewis Carroll's own quirky humour. This is a striking new edition which will make a classic story available to a new audience.

130
GREAVES, Nick
(reteller)
When Hippo Was Hairy
illustrated by Rod
Clement
Lutterworth
1988 £9.95 144pp
0 7188 2771 6

This is an excitingly different collection of stories about animals of the wild. Each of the thirty-six stories in the collection has been passed down as folk lore by different African tribes. 'The Revenge of Wild Dog' is a Ndebele story; 'Why does the Lion Roar?' is a Batonka story; there are also Zulu stories and stories from Swaziland. The stories have strongly different voices but add up to give a real feel for the animals and the countryside. Each story is illustrated by a beautiful, glossy, almost photographic full colour picture, as well as by black and white artwork. At the end of each story there is a brief factual section describing the size, eating habits, habitat and breeding of each animal.

131
HUGHES, Ted
Tales of the Early World
illustrated by Andrew
Davidson
Faber
1988 £5.95 122pp
0 571 15126 4

Ted Hughes's ten creation stories have the making of a modern mythology while remaining firmly in the tradition of other creation stories. Each story has a force and intensity that makes it seem like a truth, while also revealing an original blend of modern science and old-fashioned mysticism. Ted Hughes starts with the birds. 'Of all the birds,

Sparrow was the first to be invented. Plain little Sparrow.' But sparrow and his wife are not happy because they have no children. Sparrow decides that he must go to the top - to God himself - and ask for help. But God is busy; 'Sparrows! I can't think about Sparrows. I'm on Curlews!' he shouts. All day God works on making different birds, ending by delighting himself by creating the Swift. The cleverness of God is conveyed absolutely by Hughes, and his very human attributes make him seem most approachable. Other creatures are fashioned with less care. The Newt, for example, is plucked from the ground and then there are Leftovers, creatures like the Okapi which is made from the little bits and pieces left over in the workshop at the end of the day. Whatever the creature, Ted Hughes offers a thought-provoking, new look at the world around us in these powerfully written stories.

132
MILLER, Moira
Hamish and the Fairy Gifts
illustrated by Mairi Hedderwick
Methuen
1988 £5.50 96pp
0 416 09702 2

Moira Miller weaves fairies, ghosts and Wee Ones easily into her firmly set Scottish stories about Hamish and Mirren and their baby son. Each of the six stories, especially 'Hamish and the Fairy Bairn', is full of domestic detail, drama, local atmosphere and supernatural trickery. Written with panache and humour, *Hamish and the Fairy Gifts* is delightful entertainment.

133
OPIE, Iona
Tail Feathers From
Mother Goose
Walker
1988 £12.95 128pp
0 7445 1039 2

This is a vibrant and charming collection of some unfamiliar nursery rhymes, each illustrated by a different artist. The match between rhymes and illustrators has been carefully arranged so that it is the Victorian pinafores and ringlets of Shirley Hughes that go with 'Pedlar's Song' - 'Smiling girls, rosy boys, Here - come buy my little toys. Mighty men of gingerbread Crowd my stall with faces red; And sugar maidens you behold Lie about them all in gold.' - while Babette Cole's funny cartoon artwork gives life to 'A Rash Stipulation' - 'The daughter of a farrier Could find no one to marry her, Because she said She would not wed A man who could not carry her.' Anthony Browne, Ron Maris, Errol Le Cain, John Burningham, Helen Oxenbury and Quentin Blake are among the many other illustrators who have contributed artwork to this beautiful, enjoyable and also erudite book which is sold in aid of 'The Friends of the Bodleian Opie Appeal'.

134
PIROTTA, Saviour
(compiler)
Storyworld
illustrated by Fiona Small
Blackie
1988 £7.95 96pp
0 216 92429 4

Storyworld is a very readable collection of traditional, but not widely known stories, taken from right around the world. Each has a distinct, national voice which makes every story seem freshly told while also giving an insight into a particular culture. A short introduction at the beginning of some of the stories such as 'The Emu and the Kangaroo', an Aboriginal Dreamtime story, helps to increase understanding of different traditions of story telling.

FICTION FOR OLDER READERS

Teenage readers are capable of reading any *words* and therefore all books but they *may* enjoy messages, subjects or points of view which reflect their particular tastes. Currently, teenage fiction offers a complete slice of life - school, relationships with parents, sex, career prospects, political and social issues. The quality of writing combined with an understanding of the audience have singled these books out for selection.

135
ALCOCK, Vivien
The Trial of Anna Cotman
Methuen
1989 £7.95 172pp
0 416 13952 3

The alarming power of a gang with its secrets and sinister rituals is given full force in Vivien Alcock's exciting and tense novel. New to the town, Anna is lured into the Society of Masks by the promise of friendship with Lindy. From the beginning Anna recognises the dangers of the group, though even she has no idea just how dangerous the game is to become. The drama of *The Trial of Anna Cotman* makes it compulsive reading while the message behind it is challenging and intelligent.

136
ALLEN, Judy
Awaiting Developments
Julia MacRae
1988 £8.95 176pp
0 86203 356 X

The issues of conservation lie at the heart of *Awaiting Developments*. When Jo discovers that the house with its huge, carefully planned, old-fashioned garden is threatened by developers she feels forced to take action. Her mum and dad are sympathetic but don't wish to get involved so Jo finds that she must fight alone. Help comes from a distant relative who is staying while researching the family tree. She encourages Jo to emulate the fighting spirit of a pioneering great-great-grandmother. Jo sets to, getting up a petition from the neighbours, putting pressure on the council and tackling the developer himself. Judy Allen has written a topical and thought-provoking book.

137
ALLINGTON, Gabriel
Evacuee
Walker
1988 £7.95 176pp
0 7445 0816 9

The enormous differences between Britain and America during the war are brought sharply into focus in *Evacuee*. Gawky twelve-year-old Fanny is sent across the Atlantic for safety to stay with an unknown family, the Lippincotts. Everything about the Lippincotts and America is different from home. There is money and sophistication, both completely unfamiliar to Fanny, and lots of demonstrative affection which she finds hard to handle. But, hardest of all, she comes to learn that not all Americans are committed to helping Britain fight the war. Gabriel Allington understands Fanny's predicament completely. She tells her story with warmth while also giving insight into an unfamiliar aspect of the Second World War.

138
ASHLEY, Bernard
Bad Blood
Walker
1988 £8.95 176pp
0 86203 316 0

When Ritchie's father becomes seriously ill the only hope of saving him can come from his own family. It is up to Ritchie to discover just who that family are and why he has no previous knowledge of them. The search and the unravelling of the truth is physically tough and psychologically even tougher. Bernard Ashley writes of both with great conviction. Ritchie's pain and surprise is tangible and the final decision which he must make is handled with compassion. *Bad Blood* is an emotional novel which convinces absolutely.

139
BRANSCUM, Robbie
The Girl
Viking Kestrel
1989 £5.50 96pp
0 670 82370 8 P

The Girl is a compulsively readable domestic tragedy set in the unbearable heat of an Arkansas summer. The girl, as she is always called, and her brothers and sister live with their mean grandmother and idle grandfather. Grandma hates the children and keeps them only for the money that comes with them in the form of welfare cheques. The girl is a particular target for the grandmother's whippings as well as being prey to her uncle's lust for young girls. How she and her siblings survive by protecting each other and by keeping alive a private world is movingly told.

140
BULL, Angela
Up the Attic Stairs
Virago
1989 £3.99 232pp
1 85381 060 6 P

In *Up the Attic Stairs* Angela Bull traces the feminist movement back to its suffragette origins and, through different women from the same family in different generations, looks at what women have achieved and what they hoped to achieve. The storyline and characters are compelling and convincing from the start (although there are a lot of them and there are times when the whole structure is almost unwieldy) and the three contemporary girls provide a foreground against which the past can be set and evaluated. Angela Bull is greatly skilled at creating the atmosphere of different periods without ever resorting to obvious signposts. The terrors of marriage for girls who knew nothing of sex beforehand, the frustrations of an intelligent, principled woman doctor struggling against male prejudice, the loneliness of a woman facing life without a husband at a time when women outnumbered men but 'spinster' was still an ugly word - all of these are illustrated by the varied women whose lives are linked by Springfield, the big house on the hill.

141
BYARS, Betsy
The Burning Questions of Bingo Brown
Bodley Head
1988 £5.95 144pp
0 370 31186 8

The swiftly changing emotions of a teenager are wittily captured in *The Burning Questions of Bingo Brown*. Bingo Brown falls in love with three girls in his class all on one day and he turns himself into a handsome hulk with the help of mousse on his hair. But inside, much of him still remains a timid little boy and he certainly hasn't got the courage to lead the great T-shirt rebellion, unlike his rival Billy Wentworth. In this zippy story, full of excellent dialogue, Betsy Byars lightly unravels a first tiny love affair and its attendant problems - how do you stop holding hands with a girl, for instance? - against a fully developed background of home and parents and school and friends.

142
CORMIER, Robert
Fade
Gollancz
1988 £9.95 256pp
0 575 04402 0

Paul Moreaux inherits a strange gift from a relative. He develops the power to fade. Suddenly, he can just become invisible. At first this is a thrilling trick. Paul finds that he can be a secret witness; but as he pushes the possibilities further he finds out just how scary it can be to know more than you should. Paul struggles against the fade and wins but, as an old man, he sees the full effects of the fade on his nephew Ozzie who is almost overwhelmed by the power it exerts over him. In this dramatic, twisting and unexpected narrative Robert Cormier analyses the dangers of forbidden knowledge and shows how much in our lives is made secure by ignorance.

143
CROSS, Gillian
A Map of Nowhere
Oxford
1988 £7.95 160pp
0 19 27183 6

The sheer power of Gillian Cross' gameplaying story makes this a compulsive thriller. Nick's passion in life is playing games with a role master, tiny figures and a series of choices. When he finds Joseph's wallet in his bag and in it all the indicators that he, too, plays, Nick is determined to play with him. But Joseph's game has dimensions that Nick has never explored before. At the same time, he is being manipulated like a figure in a game by his brother who has sinister purposes of his own. *A Map of Nowhere* is a hard hitting book verging on being too violent, except that it ends with a determinedly hopeful and moral decision.

144
DAVIES, Hunter
Saturday Night
Viking Kestrel
1988 £5.50 137pp
0 670 82492 5 P

Clever and articulate Cartner reveals his life and times as a sixth former dreaming of a girl who may, or may not, be unattainable. Written as a witty first person narrative, *Saturday Night* is shrewdly observant of how parents, friends and teachers look to an adolescent.

145
DAVIS, Jenny
Sex Education
Orchard
1989 £4.95 154pp
1 85213 148 9 P

Sex Education is a strong, compulsively readable teenage romance with a serious core and an unexpectedly tragic ending. Livvie has just moved to a new school when she meets David. They go to the same biology class and quickly find that they have an unexpected amount in common. Against the background of their sex education classes, which place a heavy emphasis on caring, they quickly fall in love. Together they work on a project set by their teacher on caring for someone who needs help. Their new neighbour, Maggie, seems the ideal choice but in trying to care for her David and Livvie have taken on an impossible task. Jenny Davis writes with real understanding of how teenagers behave and think. She also shows how good intentions can go badly wrong.

146
DICKINSON, Peter
Eva
Gollancz
1988 £7.95 224pp
0 575 04354 7

After a terrible accident the only way of saving thirteen-year-old Eva is to put her mind into the body of a chimpanzee. Eva comes round from a long period of unconsciousness and must adapt to her new self. Is she a person or a chimpanzee? If she is a chimpanzee what are the implications for her and for all the other chimpanzees who are kept in the Pool? Peter Dickinson has set his novel in a future age when the earth is so heavily populated that there is no natural habitat left for animals. Within this extremely readable but disturbing book he makes a vehement case for animal liberation while also posing moral questions about the ethics of medical experiments.

147
DUDER, Tessa
Alex
Oxford
1988 £6.95 182pp
0 19 558169 5

Alex, the eponymous heroine of this story, is a potential Olympic swimmer but she is also a fifteen-year-old girl with a great many other talents and interests. Set in New Zealand in 1959 and told in the first person, *Alex* is a vigorous, dramatic and finally emotional novel, its pace set by the gruelling trials and training which Alex must push herself through. It is also much more than the story of a swim to success. Though at times Alex is irritatingly successful and selfish - ballet, music, school dramatics and school work are all done to a high standard - she is also strongminded and unconforming. Through the novel Tessa Duder touches lightly on love, sexual stereotyping and the difficulty of children doing what they want and not what their parents expect, as well as providing an insight into how champions are made.

148
FINE, Anne
Goggle-Eyes
Hamish Hamilton
1989 £7.95 144pp
0 241 12617 7

Conducted as a conversation held between two girls in a school lost property cupboard, *Goggle-Eyes* is both enormously enjoyable and deeply perceptive. Anne Fine has a sharp ear for family dialogue and a clear understanding of the complicated dynamics created by the arrival of a step-parent. In an attempt to cheer up Helly Johnson whose mother's choice of new stepfather is causing such pain, Kitty pours out her family's reaction to *their* new stepfather Gerald Faulkner, or 'goggle-eyes' as Kitty prefers to call him. The story of Kitty's intolerance, her hatred of her sister who is much more accommodating, her anger at her mother for wanting Gerald at all and then, gradually, her own capitulation into understanding, respect and even liking for him is narrated with pace and tenderness.

149
FOX, Paula
In a Place of Danger
Orchard
1989 £4.95 135pp
1 85213 166 7 P

Paula Fox's writing is cool and restrained but she tells an enormously readable story which is full of passion and also understanding. Refreshingly, it is also a book which looks at a relationship between adults from a child's perspective. While Emma's father undergoes life-saving heart surgery, Emma has to spend two weeks with her father's little known stepsister Bea and her husband Crispin. From the first Emma recognises just how difficult her stay will be. In her diary on that first day she writes, 'I'm here. Uncle Crispin is really nice although a little peculiar. The bay and the beach are great. Aunt Bea is' - but Aunt Bea's behaviour is so different that she cannot begin to describe her. During the two tense weeks Emma finds release through the tiny village she builds on the sand with the girl from next door, but all the time she is watching the strange, sad interaction between her aunt and uncle. And, when she gets home and discovers how Aunt Bea has finished the description of herself, Emma finds she can understand and forgive her.

150
GARDEN, Nancy
Annie on my Mind
Virago
1988 £3.95 240pp
0 86068 271 4 P

Nancy Garden has written a perceptive and sensitive story about two girls whose friendship becomes so close that they must acknowledge that it is sexual. Written in the first person it recalls how Liza meets Anna and how they develop a close, romantic relationship which blossoms as they spend their time exploring New York. Anna is already aware of her own sexuality and is frightened of forcing Liza into something for which she is unprepared. Liza's decision making is coloured by the attitudes of her school, whose old-fashioned moral code is judgmental and condemning.

151
GARFIELD, Leon
The Empty Sleeve
Viking Kestrel
1988 £7.95 184pp
0 670 80118 6

The dramatic variety and atmospheric intensity of *The Empty Sleeve* make it a compulsive story. Leon Garfield is simply brilliant at embroiling the reader in the unpleasant, in this case exceptionally so, intrigues of eighteenth-century life. Peter Gannet has the misfortune to be born a twin, on a snowy Saturday and when the church bells are ringing the noon chimes, thus making him a 'chime child' and the inescapable victim of ghosts. Sent as an apprentice to a locksmith in London, Peter becomes trapped in a cruel world where he is plagued by ghosts, cheats and finally, a murderer. Both the plot and the characters of *The Empty Sleeve* are multi-layered, with superstition and fantasy thickly interwoven with reality.

152
GREEN, Roger J.
The Throttlepenny
Murder
Oxford
1989 £7.95 200pp
0 19 271601 8

The Throttlepenny Murder is a hauntingly horrible story, excellently told by Roger J. Green. Set at the end of the nineteenth century, it is a complex but tidily constructed account of how a thirteen-year-old girl is accused of a murder which she hasn't committed. Jessie will hang if the truth is not told by someone. But who knows the truth and will they tell it? Though the pace of the novel is stately the tension is held absolutely. Roger J. Green has created convincing characters and set them firmly and well in an historical period. He gives good insights into what life was like for different levels of society, especially the poor.

153
HINTON, S.E.
Taming the Star Runner
Gollancz
1989 £8.95 159pp
0 575 04469 1

Full of violence and passion, *Taming the Star Runner* is a tense and compulsive story and a sympathetic one too. S.E. Hinton's writing is powerful. She uses teenage idioms to excellent effect and has a great ability to observe life with teenage eyes. Travis is a hard hero with a soft core - an angry teenager who can also write. After a violent attack on his step father he is sent right away to live with an uncle in Oklahoma. Here Travis learns that his inner self is more important than his image. He learns to be around quite different people and to understand and sympathise with their needs. His Uncle Ken, Casey who runs the stable and is controlling the wild horse Star Runner (the parallel with Travis himself is lightly enough handled), the horsey girls, Ken's ex-wife with her conventional and limited horizons, all are interesting and convincing characters from whom Travis learns about a wider kind of life.

154
HOWARD, Ellen
Edith Herself
Collins
1988 £5.95 133pp
0 00 184254 4

Edith Herself is a brief but memorable episode set in America at the end of the last century. When Edith's mother dies Edith is sent to live with her older sister and stern, school teacher brother-in-law. Edith's apprehension at the change is tangible and understandable but in fact she finds that she can adapt to their life and, more importantly, she and they and her friends all learn to cope with her epileptic fits.

155
JENKINS, Lyll
Becerra de
The Honourable Prison
Virago
1989 £3.99 199pp
1 85381 077 0 P

Lyll Becerra de Jenkins' first person narrative reveals exactly how seventeen-year-old Marta feels about the effects her father's political activities have on the daily life of the family. An outspoken journalist, his editorials against the dictator who rules their South American country lead first to a life of frightening secrets and then to a sudden, midnight intrusion when the whole family is hurried away to a remote village in the Andes where they are kept under house arrest. Every aspect of Marta's life is affected by her father's outspoken commitment, a commitment she both resents and admires. Marta's story, with its background of political turmoil and terror, gives a vivid account of the full horrors of political dictatorship.

156
JONES, Allan Frewin
Rabbit Back and
Doubled
Hodder & Stoughton
1989 £8.95 125pp
0 340 48517 5

Allan Frewin Jones has a good ear for teenage dialogue and a good eye for emerging teenage relationships. *Rabbit Back and Doubled* is a gentle romance set against a background of school, home and friendship. Tony has always been uneasy about the sex-mad, sexist attitudes of his mates but he has never had the energy to resist them. When he begins to fall in love with the unglamorous Rachel he has to make a choice and set himself apart from them. But he has Rachel.

157
KAPLAN, Bess
Rebecca Devine
Oxford
1988 £6.95 192pp
0 19 271609 3

The whirling, confused emotions of ten-year-old Rebecca are delicately and sensitively expressed in *Rebecca Devine*. Against a well-established background of a Jewish family newly emigrated to Canada in the 1930s with the attendant problems that brings, Bess Kaplan tells how Rebecca fights to keep alive the memory of her mother and resists her relatives' attempts to find a suitable step mother. Rebecca is credible and sympathetic throughout and there is enough humour in the book to make it wholly enjoyable rather than merely sentimental.

158
KAYE, Geraldine
Great Comfort
Andre Deutsch
1988 £3.50 192pp
0 233 98300 7 P

Those who enjoyed *Comfort Herself* will be delighted by this sequel which tells of Comfort's return to her father and his Ga tribe in Ghana after a two-year absence. Comfort's perceptive sense of herself and her need to belong to her English self as well as her Ghanaian self strikes a chord for everyone, even if their roots are less disparate. Her need to understand the 'not-done' things in her two, quite separate lives is sensitively explored while also giving sharp and often witty insights into our own and the Ga way of life. It is the village life in Wanwangeri where Comfort goes to visit her Grandmother that is most powerfully portrayed. Geraldine Kaye gives a clear picture of the old tribal ways - some good and some bad - and their uneasy co-existence with modern Ghana. She shows how impossible it is for Comfort to truly belong there, any more than she truly belongs in the small, parochial village in England where she lives with her English grandparents. But though Comfort does not belong exactly anywhere, *Great Comfort* is a book of enormous warmth with powerful and convincing characters. It is also a book of great perception, not only about Comfort's personal dilemma but also about society in Africa and England.

159
KENWORTHY, John
Running Riot
Viking Kestrel
1988 £3.95 74pp
0 670 82143 8 P

The tone of *Running Riot* is pleasingly light and readable but the message is a powerful and sad one. Set in a South Yorkshire mining village during the period of the miners' strike, it describes how the children in the village get caught up in the violence that erupts out of the tension of the situation. Time was that life had seemed quite boring but the strike changes all that. Now everything has an element of confrontation to it and for Goughy, previously a fairly harmless troublemaker, that confrontation escalates into danger. John Kenworthy takes his story right to its logical but tragic ending.

160
LAIRD, Christa
Shadow of the Wall
Julia MacRae
1989 £8.95 164pp
0 86203 372 1

Christa Laird's subject, the struggle for survival by Jewish children in Poland after the Nazi invasion, is an emotional one. Her creation of a fictional account of some of the things that happened is compulsive and profoundly moving. The story centres around Misha who lives in the Orphans' Home for Jewish children run by a remarkable and real character, Dr Janusk Korczak in Warsaw. Misha is responsible for his two younger sisters and also for his dying mother who lives in another part of the Jewish ghetto. Misha is only young himself but he has to take risks and make decisions which require courage and maturity. He is surrounded by others – adults and children – who must do the same. It is the solidarity of these people who remain determined against the horrors that surround them that makes *Shadow of the Wall* a book full of hope as well as tragedy.

161
LAWRENCE, Louise
Calling B for Butterfly
Bodley Head
1988 £2.95 160pp
0 370 31256 2 P

Calling B for Butterfly mixes space drama and human interest in a powerful combination. Four teenagers, a toddler and a small baby are the only survivors of an intergalactic crash in which twelve hundred people, including all their relatives, are killed. The Life Ferry is hurtling towards Jupiter. The four older children do not know how to control it or how to work the radio. Nor do they have any idea how to cope with a demanding toddler and a tiny baby. The tension between them is almost unbearable, disaster looks inevitable. And yet, they are saved by the strange music and light which comes from an unidentified source of power somewhere on board ship. Louise Lawrence provides an excellent new setting for an adventure in which the children must make life-saving decisions entirely on their own.

162
LINGARD, Joan
Rags and Riches
Hamish Hamilton
1988 £7.50 160pp
0 241 12204 X

This is an enjoyable book with very little in the way of plot or depth but with clear, likeable characters and lots of amusing incidents. Sam and her brother Seb tell the story or episodes in alternate chapters but with such similar voices that it reads fluently as one story. Their liberal, chaotic parents, Torquil and Isabella, their friends Morag and Hari and, most strongly of all, their wholly conventional, energetic but small-minded granny make up the cast. Joan Lingard makes her social comments wittily and lightly.

163
LOWRY, Lois
Anastasia Has the Answers
Armada Books
1989 £1.95 128pp
0 00 673011 6 P

Lois Lowry's Anastasia is a delightfully convincing, likeable thirteen-year-old. She's fond of her parents but also recognises that her dad is a bit of a wimp (more like Ashley Wilkes than Rhett Butler). She's aware of boys but more inclined to be influenced by her feelings for the glamorous gym teacher. Which is why she is so determined to climb one of the ropes swinging high in the gym. School, home, friends and Anastasia herself come alive in this most recent 'Anastasia' story which, like its predecessors, is eminently readable.

**164
McCAUGHREAN,
Geraldine**
A Pack of Lies
Oxford
1988 £7.95 192pp
0 19 271612 3

Alisa finds MCC Berkshire in the library by mistake. (Being in the library at all is a mistake in her opinion.) Taking MCC home seems to happen by accident but it has happened and soon he is living in the antique shop and spinning the most amazing pack of lies. The background of Alisa, her mother and the shop are thin but sound and make an easy foil for the virtuosity of MCC's inventive and stylistically varied stories. The unusual structure of *A Pack of Lies* makes it particularly enjoyable to read.

**165
MACE, Elisabeth**
Under Siege
Andre Deutsch
1988 £3.50 176pp
0 233 98345 7 P

The drama of the make-believe game that lies at the centre of *Under Siege* is intense and credible, as is Morris' involvement in it. The rest of Morris' life and the characters in it are shadowy and insubstantial. In the game that Morris plays with two adults, Uncle Patrick and his friend Ian, Elisabeth Mace has created a whole world in microcosm. For the adults it remains firmly a game but for Morris it becomes vitally important as his own life is increasingly complicated and unhappy. The strength of the game and the sense of it having a life of its own provide a compelling plot.

**166
MARSDEN, John**
So Much to Tell You
Julia MacRae
1989 £8.95 110pp
0 86203 386 1

Written in diary form as the observations of a thirteen-year-old, so scarred by her family experiences that she has become silent, *So Much to Tell You* is compulsive reading. The girl has been sent from the hospital which has failed to make any progress with her, to a boarding school where, it is hoped, the company of other, normal girls will help her to recover. Gradually, through her own observations of her school fellows and teachers and their attitudes to her, her story unfolds until its final satisfying conclusion.

167
MELNIKOFF, Pamela
Plots and Players
Blackie
1988 £7.50 180pp
0 216 92389 1

In *Plots and Players* Pamela Melnikoff gives an excellent account of how the Jewish Community lived in London during the reign of Elizabeth I. Their religion is outlawed so they must practise it in secret. For the children, like thirteen-year-old Philip, this means leading a complicated double life. Outwardly he must behave like any other schoolboy and yet he must also keep the laws of his religion. And all the time there is the risk of discovery. The two threads of the plot revolve around Philip's excursion into the world of the theatre as a young actor in Will Shakespeare's company and the imprisonment and finally execution of their friend Dr Lopez, the Queen's doctor who is accused of treason. A combination of adventure and historical detail, *Plots and Players* is also a fine observation of how a persecuted minority must live.

168
NAIDOO, Beverley
Chain of Fire
Collins
1988 £5.95 192pp
0 00 184176 9

Beverley Naidoo writes with more commitment than style, but the commitment is quite sufficient to make *Chains of Fire* an exciting and forceful book to read. Based on a true incident, it describes how the people of a small village resist the government's attempt to move them to their homeland - a barren, scrubby patch of land with tin shacks for houses. The move to resist comes mostly from a group of schoolchildren led by Taolo, whose family is already politically active, and Naledi who finds herself unexpectedly joining in. Through Naledi's eyes we learn how violently the black people, even children, are treated by the white South African government. Beverley Naidoo shows exactly what it means to a black family when their mother works as a servant for a white family, often many miles away. She shows how unevenly power is shared between blacks and whites in South Africa and how separate their lives are. *Chain of Fire* is an impassioned and provocative story of struggle.

169
OLDHAM, June
Double Take
Viking Kestrel
1988 £4.95 164pp
0 670 82088 1 P

June Oldham's writing is light and easy but the story at the heart of *Double Take* is a frightening one. The balance between the two makes the dramatic intensity especially powerful. Olivia Quinn, an unemployed actress, takes on a tiny part of a missing girl in the television reconstruction of her story. But Olivia's protestations that the part is insignificant are quickly disproved. Soon Olivia's own life seems to be under threat too.

170
ORGEL, Doris
The Devil in Vienna
Simon & Schuster
1989 £3.95 246pp
0 671 69953 9 P

The ordinary life of a thirteen-year-old Jewish girl living in Vienna begins to crumble and is eventually shattered by the national events that are overtaking her country. Inge writes a cheerful diary about her home, her loving parents, the grandfather to whom she is devoted, her school, and most of all her best friend Lieselotte. But Lieselotte is not Jewish. Her father is an active supporter of Hitler and he bans the friendship between the two girls. Gradually even Inge recognises how dangerous their friendship might be as her whole world collapses and she and her parents flee their home and escape to safety just in time. Through the eyes of a perceptive child the story of the Jews in Vienna in 1938 is brought vividly to life.

171
PATERSON, Katherine
Park's Quest
Gollancz
1989 £8.95 142pp
0 575 04487 X

Parkington Waddell Broughton's father died in the Vietnam War leaving Park with no memories but with the legacy of a shared name. Park knows little or nothing of his father. His mother can't or won't share what she knows with him so Park begins to find things out on his own. There is something about the story that isn't quite right but it is only when Park goes to visit his grandfather and meets a whole family which he didn't even know existed that he discovers the startling truth. Katherine Paterson's unravelling of a family secret is compassionate and painful.

172
PEYTON, K.M.
Downhill All the Way
Oxford
1988 £5.95 149pp
0 19 271585 2

Downhill All the Way makes an excellent antidote to books for teenagers with a serious message. Very funny in parts and highly readable throughout, it is packed full of action and characters. Jazz, David, Jean, Hoomey and Nutty each has a different reason for going on the school skiing trip and each one of them gets something different out of it. There's drama from the moment of arrival when the teacher in charge falls and breaks a leg to the last, celebratory night when the whole dining room of the chalet crashes to the ground outside. There's real terror for Jean and David when they get lost coming home in the dark, there's romance for Jean, and, running through it all, there is Hoomey's involvement in a completely ludicrous plan to outsmart Mario, the local glamour boy.

173
PHIPSON, Joan
Bianca
Viking Kestrel
1988 £4.95 138pp
0 670 82089 X P

Bianca is an adventure story with psychological overtones for teenagers which works on the strength of Joan Phipson's writing rather than on the plausibility of its plot or characters. Hubert and his sister Emily encounter a strange, frightened girl rowing on the lake. She is terrified of them but mostly she seems to be terrified of her mother. Meanwhile Hubert and Emily's father, the local doctor, is dealing with a distraught mother whose child has disappeared. The background story that unravels is fascinating and beautifully spun. It holds the reader absolutely and the final reuniting of the two is well worth waiting for.

174
PILLING, Ann
Stan
Viking Kestrel
1988 £6.95 192pp
0 670 81770 8

Stan is on the run. He runs away from his foster home because he needs the security of his own family, his only brother who he is sure will take him in. Unfortunately his break-out coincides with something much more serious and Stan is in danger of his life. He is determined to escape. His journey and the people who help him and those who stand in his way are all documented in detail so that the reader's involvement with Stan is absolute. His courage and resourcefulness are convincing even if his moral logic is a bit dubious at times. In *Stan* Ann Pilling offers a sympathetic and genuine character in a fast-moving adventure.

175
SEFTON, Catherine
The Beat of the Drum
Hamish Hamilton
1989 £7.95 105pp
0 241 12642 8

Catherine Sefton's powerful writing is an excellent match for the sombre theme of *The Beat of the Drum*. Brian Hanna is a Protestant and all his friends are mixed up in the loyalist movement - some willingly and some less so. Brian himself, though he lost his parents in a bomb blast, manages to remain a detached observer of the events around him. Loyalist tactics are no better than those of the IRA and most of the ordinary people involved on both sides are being manipulated by a system which is way beyond their control or even their comprehension. Through Brian Hanna's shrewd eyes Catherine Sefton gives an individual and wholly convincing view of the daily circumstances which surround teenagers growing up in Northern Ireland.

176
ST. GEORGE, Judith
You've Got to Believe Me
Methuen
1988 £7.95 160pp
0 416 05162 6

Against a well-set background of Cape Cod in the spring, when there are few people around and the weather is extreme, *You've Got to Believe Me* is a pacey thriller with a lot of atmosphere and a bit of romance. Recently moved to the Cape from Colorado, Matt hates everything about it - the climate and the people most especially. The only thing he enjoys is exploring the deserted marshes with the dog he walks for an old lady. Then Matt witnesses a series of unusual goings-on after a secretive couple move into one of the renting houses. Matt does everything wrong and puts himself in danger but he and Julie, who has unexpectedly become his girl friend, ultimately unravel the mystery and prove it to the police.

177
TERRIS, Susan
Nell's Quilt
Virago
1988 £3.95 176pp
0 86068 087 8 P

At the centre of *Nell's Quilt* lies the story of a young girl in 1899, who longs for a proper education and the chance of freedom, and finds herself instead committed to marrying a local widower whom her father has chosen for her. Nell apparently accepts her lot but she also makes her own way out by becoming anorexic - a then unrecognised condition. Nell keeps up a remarkable pretence of normality while slipping further and further into an unreal world centred around the quilt on which she is feverishly working. Susan Terris gives a clear insight into a world where women had few choices. Nell's self-destruction and confusion make a powerful story.

178
TOMALIN, Ruth
Long Since
Faber
1989 £6.99 112pp
0 571 15206 6

Long Since is a gentle book rich in atmosphere and flavour. In a series of interwoven chapters it describes the very different lives of some of the individual children in a tiny village community about 100 years ago. Many strands run through the story, some of which are never fully tied up - an inconsistency which, surprisingly, is satisfying rather than irritating for the reader. Ruth Tomalin's character studies, her descriptions of all things outdoors - the wild life, flowers, weather, trees, and her ability to convey a period feel with delicacy and conviction, make *Long Since* both informative and thoroughly enjoyable.

179
WARD, Glenyse
Wandering Girl
Virago
1988 £3.95 168pp
0 86068 185 8 P

Glenyse Ward's first person narrative is direct, sounding as if spoken. She tells of the life of an Aborigine girl who works as a servant for a family, where she is worked hard from dawn to dusk and treated like dirt. But the spirit of the girl remains strong. This is not a catalogue of laments but a story of how you can escape repression by sheer force of character. *Wandering Girl* makes its points about how poorly the Aborigines have been treated within the framework of a story of hope.

180
ZINDEL, Paul
A Begonia for Miss
Applebaum
Bodley Head
1989 £2.95 192pp
0 370 31268 6 P

Paul Zindel's easy style almost disguises the importance of the story he is telling. Told through the reportage of two friends, Zelda and Henry, *A Begonia for Miss Applebaum* is the account of how, on hearing of Miss Applebaum's retirement, Zelda and Henry, who have always adored her idiosyncratic and highly educational teaching, decide to take her a plant. In exchange Miss Applebaum offers to take them on an eye-opening tour of Central Park, the Museum and much more. Zelda and Henry quickly become wholly involved with Miss Applebaum. They cannot believe that she is dying of cancer and are determined to get her the best possible medical help which, they are sure, she is being denied by her small-minded relatives. But is their intervention right? Their action has repercussions which they could not have anticipated. By showing how an individual faces death, Paul Zindel sets readers thinking hard about choices in dying - and who should make them.

COLLECTIONS OF STORIES

Short stories have the special quality of conveying a message, often one with a twist or surprise, in just a brief space. They reflect a highly controlled and skilled narrative.

181
BIERMAN, Valerie (editor)
Streets Ahead
Methuen
1989 £7.95 155pp
0 416 12752 5

The stories Valerie Bierman has collected together are partly about the city, partly about the country and partly about where and how the city and country meet. 'Owls Are Night Birds' is Berlie Docherty's sensitive description of change. People change and the countryside changes and things get lost in the process. Joan Lingard is brisk and funny in her firmly Edinburgh-set story about a family trying to keep track of their bicycles in 'Bicycle Thieves'. Also set in Edinburgh, Anne Fine's 'Fight the Good Fight' is an amusing account of one girl's attempt - and success - to ban smoking on the number 14 bus. Among the other stories, Michael Hardcastle has contributed a tough footballing story and Terrance Dicks an atmospheric story of London during the Blitz as seen through the eyes of a small boy.

182
BLAKE, Jon
Showdown
Viking Kestrel
1988 £4.95 92pp
0 670 82087 3 P

The three stories in this collection are remarkably different from one another. Together they make lively and thought-provoking reading. In the title story the sight of Weevil with a brand new Yamaha is too much for Ol who challenges him to a race. But Ol doesn't have a bike to ride and when he gets one he can't ride it. It is left to Conrad to decide whether to win for him or not. In 'Why Not?' Mick takes a shoe for a walk and sets up an unlikely fashion for a village which is easily hoodwinked. Most questions are raised by 'Be Honest', an account of the disastrous things that happen to Steve when he decides to be completely honest.

183
BOWKETT, Steve
Catch
Gollancz
1988 £7.95 128pp
0 575 04399 7

The ordinary and the fantastical are woven solidly together in these nine short stories which explore how the unreal world touches the real one. Colin is warned that the desirable Eleanor is a vampire. The idea sticks. Going out with her has an unexpected and frightening quality. Steve's first real date with Hayley is spoiled by the strange thing hatching in the garden shed. Is it really a dragon struggling for existence? Stephen Bowkett shows how profoundly we are all affected by the unknown, supernatural worlds around us. He makes them as powerful and as credible as the real world of school and home and friends which he describes so well.

184
BRANFIELD, John
The Day I Shot My Dad
Gollancz
1989 £8.95 160pp
0 575 04486 1

The shooting in the title story of this collection is shooting with the camera, but the pun is a clever one reflecting the underlying theme of the collection, which is teenagers getting away from their parents' influences and proving themselves capable of independent thought, skills and relationships. John Branfield's tone and style are mild but the emotions he touches are strong ones. In 'Wet Bob, Dry Bob' Dave is determined to choose his own sport rather than follow his father's lead, but he needs his father to take it seriously too, to give it validity. John in 'The Day I Shot My Dad' has to take action to ensure that his filming project remains his own and is not taken over by his less competent father. Other stories reflect different angles on the same theme of unravelling the threads of childhood.

185
CHAMBERS, Aidan
(compiler)
Love All
Bodley Head
1988 £3.95 160pp
0 370 31206 6 P

Love All is an excellent and invigorating collection of stories. The different voices of the writers ensure that it has many tones as well as covering aspects of love which show how close love is to all kinds of other emotions. Toeckey Jones touches on an innocent but forbidden relationship between a white boy and the young black girl who is employed to nurse him. Jan Mark takes a look back at the feelings of a now middle-aged man who treated the girl who loved him with disdain. Donu Kogbara shows that being loved is part of belonging, thus being the salvation from rejection. Aidan Chambers himself tells a wicked and black story of a girl's exploitation of a boy's love. These serious stories are interspersed with some lighter touches provided by Margaret Mahy and Hunter Davies.

186
FORWARD, Toby
Pictures
Simon & Schuster
1989 £3.50 128pp
0 671 69992 X P

Toby Forward's twelve stories touch lightly but with insight on powerful and confusing emotions. Amina struggles to work out right and wrong in a world where her picture of an Asian Virgin Mary is 'too good' to hang on the wall at school but so sacrilegious at home that it is torn into strips and put in the bin. Micky's and Patch's need for thrills leads to joy-riding and death. They have their excitement and become the heroes they want to be but was it what they really meant? Geoff watches his mother dying and learns of the anger and terror that brings. Fatima learns to be loved but the love costs her her family. *Pictures* gives insights into the world of Asian girls and white boys.

187
JONES, Diana Wynne (editor)
Hidden Turnings
Methuen
1989 £8.95 184pp
0 416 11272 2

Subtitled 'A collection of stories through time and space' this is a volume of stories that will surprise and provoke. Though each has a different starting point, some in the past and some in the future, some funny and some sad, they all have an unexpected twist which makes them dynamic to read. Douglas Hill, Tanith Less, Robert Westall and Diana Wynne Jones herself are among the contributors.

188
MARK, Jan
Enough is Too Much
Already
Bodley Head
1988 £2.95 160pp
0 370 31094 2 P

Jan Mark has an exceptional ear for dialogue. Using speech with the lightest of touches she conveys mood, place and, most powerfully of all, the interaction between teenagers. She also has an ability to capture the absurd. Here, three friends discuss themselves, their feelings, relatives and much more in seven elliptical, zany episodes.

189
MASTERS, Anthony
(editor)
Taking Root
Methuen
1988 £7.95 128pp
0 416 10782 6

Anthony Masters' collection of stories is designed to show how it feels to be part of our multicultural community. Each of the authors has written a story which reflects some aspect of a particular culture. The feeling of differences between the cultures is powerfully conveyed and there is no backing away from the problems of prejudice of all kinds. Ruskin Bond's 'The Flute Player' tells of a young girl's uncertainty about whether India, which she visits every summer, or England, where she lives, is home. Gillian Klein shows just how thin the veneer of racial tolerance can be in 'The Dumper', while in 'Colour Blind' Bernard Kops reveals the extent of unthinking, deep-rooted racial prejudice and exposes it in its full horror. The greatest impact of all comes from Ron Morton's 'The Blue Chevrolet'. Here the friendship of two boys is split apart by the bigotry of an adult.

190
PRINCE, Alison
A Haunting Refrain
Methuen
1988 £7.95 128pp
0 416 05322 X

The title of this collection is a clever use of words since the haunting in each story is musical. In 'The Black Dress' Selina, wearing an old dress which she has bought from a jumble sale, hears music coming from the disused ballroom at the end of the pier and finds herself dancing a foxtrot with a handsome young man badly scarred by a German bayonet. How it happens she never really knows but the memory of the music lingers distinctly. In each of the other five stories music from the past leads a child back into another time. Alison Prince's stories are gentle and her hauntings appear as a natural extension of life rather than as something sinister.

191
SALWAY, Lance
The Darkness Under
the Stairs
illustrated by Warron
Prentice
Lutterworth
1988 £7.95 128pp
0 7188 2702 3

Lance Salway makes the settings for his ghost stories so beguilingly domestic and harmless that the element of fear, when it is produced, is especially dramatic. In the title story Andrew hears strange crying from under the neighbours' stairs and only discovers, too late, that it is himself who is crying. An argumentative family holiday in Italy sets the scene for Ben's narrow escape from the early death which the ghostly Louisa seems to have in mind for him. Into each of these well-shaped stories Lance Salway weaves a chilling strand.

192
STONES, Rosemary
(compiler)
Someday My Prince Will
Not Come
Piccadilly
1988 £6.50 94 pp
1 85340 021 1

This is a collection of stories designed to show girls the choices they have and the control they can exert over their own lives. In 'A Family Likeness' Jacqueline Roy's Livy is determined to prove that her father's talents will be inherited and remembered through her. Sandra Chick shows sharply the gulf between the assumptions of the sexes in 'Different Rules'. Suniti Namjoshi's 'Three Fables' take a light and amusing look at how women in traditional stories can get the upper hand of role playing men.

193
WATSON, James
Make Your Move
Gollancz
1988 £7.95 160pp
0 575 04397 0

All of the nine stories in James Watson's collection are vigorously written. Each revolves around the need for the individual to be independent and free thinking. The message is that tyranny, whether it's the tyranny of the secret police or Zelda's father in 'Choices', or the young child in 'The Eyes Have It', must be resisted. Just as Jan must resist the tyranny of prejudice and stereotyped thinking that may bar her from her favourite sport. Diverse in settings and characters, this is a collection which derives power from its message.

FAIRY TALES, FOLK TALES, MYTHS AND LEGENDS

Most of our traditions of storytelling come from the fairy stories and folk stories that have been preserved and handed down from one generation to another. The following collections offer a rich heritage from different cultures and different times.

194
ALEXANDER, Pat
(retold by)
The Young Puffin Book of
Bible Stories
illustrated by Anthony Kerins
Puffin
1988 £2.50 192pp
0 14 032448 8 P

The language used in Pat Alexander's retellings of over fifty of the most famous Bible stories is everyday, which means that the stories must be carried by their content. There is action in the fight between David and Goliath and in the story of the siege of Jericho; domestic drama in the squabbling between Jacob and Esau and in the judgement Solomon makes between the two women who are fighting over one baby; and tenderness in Moses and the bulrushes and in some of the parables from the New Testament. Those who know the language of the Bible will miss it but the simple style adopted here will make these stories available to a wide audience who might otherwise miss them altogether.

195
ANDERSEN, Hans
CORRIN, Stephen
(translator)
Tales from Hans Andersen
illustrated by Edward Ardizzone
Andre Deutsch
1989 £4.50 191pp
0 233 98372 4 P

'The Ugly Duckling', 'The Emperor's New Clothes', 'The Tinder Box' and 'The Little Mermaid' are among the fourteen stories by Hans Andersen selected and illustrated by Edward Ardizzone. Edward Ardizzone chose his own favourite stories for this collection and his illustrations show his delight in the stories and so enhance the reader's enjoyment of them. Stephen Corrin's translation has kept closely to the original, reflecting Hans Andersen's spare and unsentimental style.

196
APPIAH, Peggy
The Pineapple Child and other Tales from Ashanti
illustrated by Mora Dickson
Andre Deutsch
1989 £4.50 173pp
0 233 98371 6 P

Peggy Appiah's wonderfully readable collection of stories from Ghana are full of magic and animals as well as giving a strong sense of Ashanti life. Animal myths appear in, among others, 'Why the Dog Hates the Cat', 'Why the Crow has a White Neck and a Black Body', and 'Why Cat Always Chases Mouse'. Ashanti culture is reflected in other stories such as 'Why the Ashantis dislike Contradiction', 'How Death came back to Life', and in the story of the Pineapple Child herself.

197
BAYNES, Pauline (illustrator)
Noah and the Ark
Methuen
1988 £5.95 32pp
0 416 02662 1

Using the text of the Revised Standard Version of the Bible this is an atmospheric, authentic and highly readable introduction to the story of Noah which is given vigorous life by Pauline Baynes's brilliantly coloured and inspiring illustrations. Drawn in the style of illuminations for a manuscript, the illustrations have a simplicity which makes them especially fitting for the Biblical text. At the same time they are full of detail which makes them repay repeated and careful looking.

198
CORRIN, Sara (retold by)
CORRIN, Stephen (retold by)
The Pied Piper of Hamelin
illustrated by Errol Le Cain
Faber
1988 £6.95 32pp
0 571 13762 8

The familiar story of the Piper who leads away all the children of Hamelin when he is cheated out of his fee for catching rats is retold in a straightforward and easy-to-read style by Sara and Stephen Corrin. The details and atmosphere of the story are fleshed out and brought vividly to life by Errol Le Cain's busy and decorative illustrations.

199
CORRIN, Sara (retold by)
CORRIN, Stephen (retold by)
The Faber Book of Favourite Fairy Tales
illustrated by Juan Wijngaard
Faber
1988 £9.95 256 pp
0 571 14854 9

Sara Corrin is an inspiring storyteller, Stephen Corrin is a gifted translator. Between the two of them they have taken fairy stories from all traditions - 'Cinderella' from Perrault, 'Rapunzel' and 'Hansel and Gretel' from The Brothers Grimm, 'The Princess and the Pea' from Hans Christian Andersen, 'Aladdin and the Wonderful Lamp' from The Arabian Nights, 'Baba Yaga, the Bony-legged, the Witch' from Aleksandr Afanasiev, among the twenty-six - and retold them with great freshness and life. The result is a collection which will serve either as an excellent introduction for those unfamiliar with the best of the fairy tale tradition or as an exciting variant for those who already know and love them.

200
CROUCH, Marcus
Ivan: Stories of Old Russia
illustrated by Bob Dewar
Oxford
1989 £7.95 78pp
0 19 274135 7

Fifteen stories about Ivan, a universal Russian hero who appears sometimes as a simpleton and sometimes as a Prince. Marcus Crouch's retellings of these stories are contemporary in language while also capturing the traditions of Russian storytelling.

201
DICKINSON, Peter
Merlin Dreams
illustrated by Alan Lee
Gollancz
1988 £9.95 176pp
0 575 03962 0

Steeped in the traditions of the Arthurian legends, *Merlin Dreams* is a beautifully written new mythology, one that is rich in atmosphere, language and invention. Peter Dickinson imagines the aged Merlin, entombed under a great rock in the middle of a wasted moor, dreaming of the past. Each of his dreams tells the story of some quasi-Arthurian fantasy - a Knight's unwilling combat with a mysterious, shadowy enemy; a young girl's summoning of magic powers to avenge her father's death; a simple village's humanity in taking in a strange girl creature with one foot. Mystery, magic and medieval customs are blended together in these vivid fantasy legends.

202
GRAY, J.E.B. (reteller)
Indian Folk Tales and
Legends
illustrated by Joan
Kiddell-Monroe
Oxford
1989 £3.95 240pp
0 19 274138 1 P

This is a rich collection of all manner of Indian stories. There are love stories; animal fables with clear, underlying morals; tales of demons and spirits; funny stories and sad stories. Together they reflect many of the preoccupations of Indian culture as well as bringing the countryside and the birds and beasts within it vividly to life.

203
LAWRENCE, Ann
(translator)
Tales From Perrault
illustrated by Tony James
Chance
Oxford
1988 £7.95 117pp
0 19 274533 6

The eleven stories in this collection have been carefully chosen to include old favourites such as the blood-curdling 'Bluebeard' and the romantic 'The Little Glass Slipper' as well as less well-known stories like 'Riguet the Tuft' and 'The Ridiculous Wishes'. Anne Lawrence's translations are easy to read aloud while retaining a feeling for the stories' traditional nature. Surrounding the stories there is some historical background information about how Perrault came to write them for a little girl spending her summers in the country away from Paris.

204
LEWIS, Naomi
(translator)
Proud Knight, Fair Lady
illustrated by Angela
Barrett
Hutchinson
1989 £10.95 100pp
0 09 173511 4

Naomi Lewis has translated twelve stories from the minstrels of the twelfth century into rich and lyrical prose. The stories tell of a world of chivalry and courtly love, of knights and damsels and some strange intrigues. Together with Angela Barrett's illustrations they recreate the feel of another world and time.

205
LISTER, Robin (reteller)
The Story of King Arthur
illustrated by Alan Baker
Kingfisher
1988 £7.95 96pp
0 86272 333 7

For this handsome new version of some of the stories of the legendary King Arthur and his Knights of the Round Table, Robin Lister has drawn on many original sources. Starting by setting the scene with stories of Merlin the wizard, dragons and all kinds of goings-on in the country before Arthur is born, he then tells some of the most famous Arthurian stories - the young Arthur plucking the sword from the stone, the sword Excalibur rising from the lake, the search for the Holy Grail, and many more. The text is easy to read (sometimes even a little too contemporary in feel) and the illustrations are richly atmospheric.

206
McCAUGHREAN,
Geraldine
Saint George and the
Dragon
illustrated by Nicki Palin
Oxford
1989 £5.95 32pp
0 19 279793 X

How the knight George slew a fearsome dragon, thus saving a beautiful princess from certain death and a whole town from tyranny, is lyrically retold by Geraldine McCaughrean. Her story is well fleshed out and she also explains how St. George became the patron saint of England and where some of the myths about St. George originated.

207
McGOWAN, Hugh
Leprechauns, Legends
and Irish Tales
illustrated by Peter Haigh
Gollancz
1988 £10.95 128pp
0 575 04261 3

This is a sophisticated collection of Irish folk stories, most of which are about leprechauns but also including stories of the Fir Darrig, or Red Man, who is best known as the person who will always grant three wishes; the Pooka who is a sinister creature able to assume any shape at any time, and the Banshee whose terrible wail is a sure warning of death. Hugh McGowan makes the characters vivid and alive. There is little room to doubt any stories about Irish fairies after reading this collection of facts(?) and fiction about them. Peter Haigh's illustrations capture the same spirit as the text though the two are rather unsatisfactorily fitted together on the page.

208
MOSLEY, Francis
Jason and the Golden
Fleece
Andre Deutsch
1988 £5.95 32pp
0 233 98325 2

This is a jolly, straightforward version of the story of Jason setting off to get the Golden Fleece which will give him the right to wear his father's crown. The text is full of fresh dialogue and Francis Mosley's illustrations are light and airy. Both text and illustrations also capture the fearful journey across the Aegean, especially the squeeze through the narrow, towering rocks; the taming of the bulls; and the final snatching of the fleece from the ferocious dragon who never sleeps.

209
REEVES, James (reteller)
English Fables and Fairy Stories
Illustrated by Joan Kiddell-Monroe
Oxford
1989 £3.95 234pp
0 19 274137 3 P

James Reeves was a gifted storyteller and his versions of these traditional English tales - 'Jack and the Beanstalk', 'Tom Tit Tot', 'Dick Whittington and his Cat' to name a few out of the nineteen included - are fresh, spirited and retold savouring all the humour within them.

210
TADJO, Veronique
Lord of the Dance
A. & C. Black
1988 £5.95 32pp
0 7136 3051 5

The story of the Lord of the Dance is known through the familiar hymn. Here the background to the story is told. The Mask, as the Lord of the Dance is known, comes down among men and women to share in each joy and sorrow. He is celebrated by the many different masks that are made. But then, as times change, he is obscured by the coming of cities and concrete and cars. Yet, all the time, he is still there and this poem reminds children of the Senufo people that they should never forget The Mask, The Lord of the Dance. Veronique Tadjo's poem is both rhythmic and lyrical. Her illustrations are bold and primitive. The book ends with an explanation of the Mask customs among the Senufo people who live in the Ivory Coast.

POETRY

The quality and diversity of poetic forms that are currently available to children is exceptional. So not only can children enjoy the poetry that is offered to them, they will also develop the habit of enjoying poetry - once considered a rarefied taste.

211
BERRY, James
When I Dance
illustrated by Sonia Boyce
Hamish Hamilton
1988 £6.95 96pp
0 241 12426 3

James Berry's poems are evocative, lyrical inspiring and refreshingly different both from other poems and from each other. In his introduction James Berry writes that the poems draw from the rural Caribbean and from the inner-city life of London. They reflec different cultures and different ways of life but, as a unifying feature, they all ask the reader to consider and understand an aspec of life. By changing styles, rhythms and voice: James Berry is able to elicit a wide range o responses from his readers. His collectior brings a serious and powerful voice to poetr) for children.

212
COPE, Wendy (editor)
Is That the New Moon?
illustrated by Christine Roche
Lions
1989 £2.25 128pp
0 00 673240 2 P

Wendy Cope's anthology offers a most excit ing choice of poetry. Her selection is easy tc read and comprehend but its impact is power ful whether it is dipped into or read in grea gulps, which is made tempting by the unaus tere paperback format in which it is published The poems are all by women poets and mos are contemporary. Women's attitudes to them selves and to men, their feelings, how girl: react to different things are all explored anc celebrated in this brilliant anthology.

213
EDWARDS, Richard
A Mouse in My Roof
illustrated by Venice
Orchard
1988 £7.95 76pp
1 85213 133 0

A Mouse in My Roof is a collection of easy-to-read verse about everyday things. Richard Edward's amusement in the world around him is reflected in his poems. 'Dashing Away' shows how it might feel to be two creases about to be flattened by an iron. In 'Lost and Found' a boy tries to help his grandfather find the thing beginning with T which he has lost, only to discover that it is 'temper' which is lashed out on him. The light, rhythmic structure of the poems matches their content well.

214
FOSTER, John (compiler)
Another First Book of
Poetry
Oxford
1988 £5.95 126pp
0 19 917120 3

John Foster has put together a diverse collection of poems which make a good introduction to easy-to-read, home/school poetry. The collection is strongly contemporary and largely lightweight. Martin Honeysett's 'Put the Cat Out', Sheila Simmons's 'Slide', Felice Holman's 'Sulk' - poems such as these make easy verse out of the ordinary, everyday events that take place in all of our lives and do much to demystify the art of poetry.

215
FOSTER, John (compiler)
School's Out!
illustrated by Alastair
Graham
Oxford
1988 £3.95 128pp
) 19 276078 5 P

John Foster's collection of poems about school is enormously rich and varied and offers interesting and surprising angles on everything and anything to do with school. It has been divided into sections such as 'Scoo-wool - the hippiest time of your life' and 'Beware of the history teacher', but it is really a book that it is fun to dip into regardless of section. There's the pathos of Nigel Cox's 'New Boy', uneasy in an unfamiliar uniform, being left behind to board. Playtimes are summed up variously by, among others, Wes Magee in 'Morning Break' and Gregory Harrison in 'Playtime - staying in', while the unfairness of being picked for a team - or not - is captured absolutely by both Allan Ahlberg and Michael Rosen. *School's Out!* is a collection for every classroom.

216
HARRIS, Rosemary
(compiler)
Love and the Merry
Go Round
illustrated by Pauline
Baynes
Hamish Hamilton
1988 £7.95 87pp
0 241 12412 3

As the title of this selection suggests, the poems included are largely about love, or at least about people and the different relationships they have. That does not imply that it is a sentimental or slushy collection. Stevie Smith's 'My Hat' begins 'Mother said if I wore this hat, I should be certain to get off with the right sort of chap' and continues in the same amusing vein. In contrast is Edwin Muir's 'For Ann Scott-Moncrieff' which eloquently expresses what the author felt on the death of a great and much loved friend, emotions with which readers can easily identify. Siegfried Sassoon, Robert Graves and Laurie Lee are just some of the other poets included in this refreshingly unfamiliar collection.

217
HARRISON, Michael
(selector)
Splinters
illustrated by Sue Heap
Oxford
1988 £4.95 128pp
0 19 276072 6

Michael Harrison's selection of the briefest of poems makes an enormous impact. He has selected from a wide range of poets: Robert Herrick, Ezra Pound, Ogden Nash, William Wordsworth, Michael Rosen and Robert Louis Stevenson, to name but a few. He has chosen poems that are funny, sad, silly and serious. Their unifying factor is that they are short, making their points quickly and sharply. By selecting poems which are not especially well known and offering them in an unpretentious way, Michael Harrison gives everyone the chance of discovering - and remembering - some exciting and unfamiliar verse.

The Mermaid

Say not the mermaid is a myth,
I knew one once named Mrs Smith.
She stood while playing cards or knitting;
Mermaids are not equipped for sitting.

Ogden Nash

218
HARRISON, Michael
STUART-CLARK,
Christopher
The Oxford Treasury of
Children's Poems
Illustrated by Sue
Scullard
Oxford
1988 £8.95 172pp
0 19 276055 6

This is a solid collection of almost two hundred poems, some written expressly for children and some which children will enjoy anyway, taken from all different times. There are traditional rhymes such as the brief resumé of a man's life, 'Solomon Grundy', as well as old favourites like A. A. Milne's 'Disobedience' and Robert Louis Stevenson's 'My Shadow'. Contemporary poets John Agard, Michael Rosen, Kit Wright and Charles Causley are also well represented. Though the collection is presented without themes or groupings it has clearly been carefully ordered so that there are some neat juxtapositions of style and content. The illustrations are sometimes an asset, as in the simple boiled egg which accompanies Russell Hoban's 'Egg-Thoughts', but sometimes they are rather overwhelming.

219
HUDSON, Edward
(selector)
Poetry of the First World War
Wayland
1988 £8.95 128pp
1 85210 667 0

The careful ordering of the poems in this collection and the intelligent use of photographs to illustrate them, ensures that this collection makes a powerful impact. Each year of the war is reflected by the poems written in it, thus it is easy to get a feel of the changing mood of contemporary reaction to it. The spirit of optimism and patriotism that lies behind W. N. Hodgson's opening poems is completely missing from Leslie Coulson's angry 'Who Made the Law?' written in 1916. 'Who made the Law that men should die in meadows? Who spake the word that blood should splash in lanes?' By 1918 Wilfred Owen and Siegfried Sassoon were offering a picture of the realities of war which could no longer be ignored by those at home. The inclusion of some poems written in the 1920s shows too that memories of the war did not just disappear, nor was the war itself forgotten. Edward Hudson's collection will bring the First World War vividly, almost too vividly, alive for a new generation.

220
McGOUGH, Roger
An Imaginary Menagerie
illustrated by Tony Blundell
Viking Kestrel
1988 £6.95 108pp
0 670 82330 9

Through his inventive poems, written from A-Z, Roger McGough gives unexpected insights into some familiar animals as well as creating some wholly original ones. Most of the poems are slightly trivial but the overall effect is entertaining and the collection reflects a great many different kinds of verse.

221
MAGEE, Wes
Morning Break and Other Poems
illustrated by Valerie Patrone
Cambridge
1989 £2.25 64pp
0 521 36940 1 P

Wes Magee's poems are easy to read and easy to enjoy. This collection is built around the immediate world of children - home, family relations, school and the major celebrations of bonfire night and Christmas. There is little to challenge or surprise here but the sheer accessibility of the verse gives value to the collection.

222
NICHOLLS, Judith
(selector)
Wordspells
illustrated by Alan Baker
Faber
1988 £7.95 144pp
0 571 14891 3

This collection will serve as an introduction to many different poetic styles. Judith Nicholls has selected her poems widely and with care. She has included many scant verses which in their few lines can say as much as a whole story. She has also included story poems, musical poems and traditional sayings and rhymes. Alan Baker's beautiful line illustrations enhance the mood and atmosphere of the poems they illustrate.

223
NICHOLLS, Judith
(editor)
What on Earth . . . ?
illustrated by Alan Baker
Faber
1989 £7.95 118pp
0 571 15261 9

The subtitle of this collection, 'Poems with a Conservation Theme', explains the basis for inclusion, while the poems themselves show just what a good theme it is. There are poems from all around the world, from times past as well as from today, reflecting that what man is doing to nature is a universal and timeless problem. The comments of John Clare, William Blake and William Wordsworth have every bit as much relevance as those of John Updike, Pete Seeger or Roger McGough. Judith Nicholls has put together a collection that combines beautiful poetry with much scope for thought.

The Inheritor

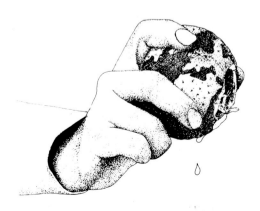

224
NICHOLS, Grace
Come on into my
Tropical Garden
illustrated by Caroline
Binch
A. & C. Black
1988 £5.95 42pp
0 7136 2989 4

Grace Nichols' poems are elegant. They are also evocative, giving clear impressions of people, places, birds, animals and a way of life in the Caribbean. The poems, from the title poem onwards, are written with the clear intention of revealing the delights of the Caribbean to those who do not know it. Grace Nichols welcomes readers, drawing them kindly to her own culture. Caroline Binch's fine line drawings match the mood and the subjects well.

225
NICHOLS, Grace
(compiler)
Black Poetry
illustrated by Michael
Lewis
Blackie
1988 £6.95 144pp
0 216 92430 8

Grace Nichols has deliberately chosen to define black poetry as widely as possible so as to include white poets who speak with the voice of the Caribbean and Asian poets, who do not necessarily fit the traditional black image but whose poems express the feelings of a minority culture. Above all this is a vibrant, diverse and exciting collection which, by including poems with a powerful and authentic voice, introduces subjects and language which are rarely represented in poetry.

226
O'CALLAGHAN, Julie
Taking My Pen For a
Walk
Orchard
1988 £6.95 96pp
1 85213 109 8

Julie O'Callaghan's poems are original, provocative and fun to read. In poems such as 'Happy Birthday from Bennigans' she reflects a teenager's humiliation and contempt as the waitress bursts into song for her birthday. In 'Moving House' her brief, eleven line poem expresses exactly what it feels like to pack everything up and leave a place you know forever. In both language and content Julie O'Callaghan speaks directly to teenagers.

227
PRELUTSKY, Jack
Tyrannosaurus Was a
Beast
illustrated by Arnold
Lobel
Julia MacRae
1988 £6.95 32pp
0 86203 371 3

Fourteen funny poems provide a great deal of interesting information about different kinds of dinosaurs. 'Tyrannosaurus was a beast/That had no friends to say the least./It ruled the ancient out-of-doors,/And slaughtered other dinosaurs.' Other, less well-known dinosaurs - the Allosaurus, the Quetzalcoatlus and the Seismosaurus, for example - are included too. Arnold Lobel's realistic illustrations match the spirit of the text exactly.

228
SCHENK de REGNIERS,
Beatrice
MOORE, Eva
WHITE, Mary Michaels
CARR, Jan
Sing a Song of Popcorn
Hodder & Stoughton
1988 £8.95 160pp
0 340 49078 0

Despite its lightweight title this is a good and enjoyable collection of poems for young children, richly illustrated throughout. For convenience, it has been divided into nine themed sections - 'spooky poems', 'story poems', 'mostly nonsense' and so on - and each section has its own illustrator whose pictures reflect the theme well. Maurice Sendak's illustrations to the story poems are particularly effective. Favourites from Ogden Nash, Robert Louis Stevenson and Edward Lear are included as well as many less familiar verses which stand well alongside.

229
SILVERSTEIN, Shel
A Giraffe and a Half
Cape
1988 £5.95 48pp
0 224 02612 7

Shel Silverstein's particular brand of zany humour is shown off to excellent effect in *A Giraffe and a Half*. 'If you had a giraffe . . . and he stretched another half . . . you would have a giraffe and a half.' And the illustrations show it to be so. Throughout the forty-eight pages the giraffe poem is stretched to its full extent as a series of hilarious things happen and are piled up on the giraffe.

230
THOMPSON, Brian
Catch It If You Can
illustrated by Susie
Jenkin-Pearce
Viking Kestrel
1989 £6.95 32pp
0 670 82279 5

Some favourite and familiar rhymes - 'Humpty Dumpty' and 'Round and Round the Garden' - are joined by less well-known but equally rhythmic and simple verses for the very young. Each poem has bright and cheerful illustrations to make the collection into an attractive picture book.

231
WILSON, Raymond
(selector)
Every Poem Tells a Story
illustrated by Alison
Darke
Viking Kestrel
1988 £6.95 166pp
0 670 82086 5

The enormous range of poems in this collection shows that you can tell all kinds of stories in all kinds of poetic forms. Raymond Wilson starts with the story of emotion, 'A Poison Tree' by William Blake - 'I was angry with my friend: I told my wrath, my wrath did end.' He goes on to include the dramatic 'Lord Randal', poisoned and weary and ready to die, and the macabre and witty 'The Dorking Thigh' by William Plomer. Funny, sad, well-known and obscure, this is an interesting and intelligent collection for older readers with a strong, unifying theme.

The world around us and the people who have contributed to it in the past and are doing so in the present are described in some detail in the books below. In some cases it is the special contribution that an individual has made that is considered, while in others it is the importance of other cultures and ways of life.

232
BLACKWOOD, Alan
Twenty Tyrants
illustrated by Edward
Mortelmans
Wayland
1989 £6.50 48pp
1 85210 140 7

The brief account of what a tyrant is, and how he or she may have come to be one, sets the scene for simplified but informative biographies of tyrants ranging from Herod the Great and Queen Boudicca, through Emperor Nero, Attila the Hun and Henry VIII, on to more recent figures such as Adolf Hitler and Joseph Stalin, and right up to the present day with the inclusion of Pol Pot and Jean Bedel Bokassa. Tyranny may be in the eye of the beholder but certainly all those included here justify their name.

233
CHARLTON, Michael
Wheezy
Bodley Head
1988 £5.95 32pp
0 370 31150 7

Michael Charlton's story describes what it feels like to suffer from asthma and what you can do to overcome it. The combination of its storyline about William learning to do more and more things, especially sports, and his own project about his medicines and the things he does to avoid asthma attacks makes this optimistic fiction into a book full of facts too.

234
CLEMENTS, Gillian
The Truth about Castles
Macmillan
1988 £5.95 32pp
0 333 47067 2

What looks like a cartoon book is, in fact, a very serious introduction to everything you need to know about castles. The contents list covers Building a Castle, Inside the Castle, The Concentric Castle, Defending Castles, Attacking Castles and Castles in Decline and, through her witty but wholly accurate illustrations and their brief captions, Gillian Clements describes all these things. Gillian Clements has made the building of castles and living in them seem real.

235
CRESSWELL, Helen
The Story of Grace
Darling
Puffin
1988 £1.75 72pp
0 14 032434 8 P

The story of Grace Darling is extraordinary as much for how Grace's one act of enormous heroism was received as for the act itself. Grace Darling was the daughter of the lighthouse keeper of the Longstone Light on the wild Northumberland coast. Her whole life was spent on remote, sea-washed spots helping her father to keep the light burning. Her brothers helped her father with wrecks but Grace, as a mere girl, was never expected to do so until the fateful day in 1838 when the *Forfarshire* foundered in heavy seas when only Grace was at home to help. Thereafter the public took Grace up as a national heroine showering her with gifts, and idolising her courage. Helen Cresswell tells Grace's story against a powerfully conveyed feeling for the unusual way of life she lived.

236
CUMMING, David
India
photographs by Jimmy
Holmes
Wayland
1989 £7.50 48pp
0 85078 966 4

With a country as large and diverse as India it is hard to do more than briefly introduce different aspects of life in different parts of the country. David Cumming does that well, touching on climate, wild life, religion, language, life in the town and life in the country, sports and pastimes and taking a brief look ahead at the future of the country. His text is packed with information and is interesting to read. Jimmy Holmes's photographs illuminate the points well.

237
GIBSON, Michael
Warfare in the
Twentieth Century
Wayland
1989 £7.50 32pp
1 85210 398 1

Lest anyone forget, this book shows clearly just how terrible are all forms of warfare from the simplest soldiering of the late nineteenth century, through the advancing technology of machine guns, the coming of tanks, submarines and sophisticated aeroplanes to the literally devastating possibility of total war. Michael Gibson gives some background details on how the major wars of the past have come about as well as offering information on some of the other aspects of war such as spying and terrorism.

238
HEATER, Derek
Refugees
Wayland
1988 £6.50 46pp
1 85210 436 8

Derek Heater traces the history of refugees in the past and looks at the lives of some present-day refugees. He explains the many reasons which may have caused people to flee their homelands and how badly on the whole they have been received by the countries they have fled to. He also describes how the refugees live, work and fight for survival and how and what aid can be provided to help them. The text of *Refugees* combines a great deal of technical information with sympathetic insights into the plight of millions of people throughout the world. Simple maps reinforce the factual side of the book as photographs do the human side.

239
HUNTER, Mollie
Flora Macdonald and
Bonnie Prince Charlie
illustrated by Chris
Molan
Methuen
1988 £4.95 32pp
0 416 06212 1

Flora Macdonald, who usually appears as a shadowy and rather insubstantial figure in the story of Bonnie Prince Charlie's escape to Skye, is here shown playing a prominent part. Not only does she take an active role in helping the prince with his disguise - she refuses to let him carry a pistol under his dress, for example - but she also uses her feminine charms to distract one of the redcoats at dinner so that the prince can be helped to safety. Mollie Hunter tells the romantic story with style and relish. By giving a lot of details she makes the escape from South Uist to Skye historically alive.

240
KABEER, Naila
Anu in Bangladesh
photographs by
Prodeepta
Das
A. & C. Black
1988 £4.50 25pp
0 7136 2979 7

Twelve-year-old Anu describes her life in Bangladesh. The text has been cleverly created so that all aspects of life are touched on. Anu and her family live a city life in Dhaka. Their flat, their clothes, how they shop, where Anu's father works, their worship, their cooking and their play are all described by Anu and illustrated by Prodeepta Das's striking photographs. Life in the country is discussed, too, as Anu's grandmother lives in a village which can only be reached by boat. Text and photographs combine to give a clear impression of what someone else's life is like.

241
KNIGHT, Julia
Book Publishing
Wayland
1988 £6.95 48pp
1 85210 239 X

In *Book Publishing* a comprehensive history of printing, publishing and the role the book has played in society, and especially in education, is followed by chapters on fiction, non-fiction, the structure of publishing and a look at some *causes célèbres*. Julia Knight's text is crammed with detailed information and is particularly enlightening on the finer points of publishing today and how it may develop in the future.

242
KRAMER, Ann
Women and Politics
Wayland
1988 £6.95 48pp
1 85210 388 4

Ann Kramer traces the history of women's first impact on politics in the early nineteenth century through to the present day and even takes a look at what might happen in the future. Women's active involvement in politics took a long time coming and depended on the campaigning strengths of various key individuals whose achievements in raising the status and command of women is documented here. Crucial achievements and setbacks in the movement are also described and explained.

243
LEYSER, Henrietta
Medieval Women
Oxford
1988 £4.95 32pp
0 19 913347 6

Though called *Medieval Women* this is really a look at what options women had in Medieval times compared with what is now available for them. The stories from those times of women and marriage, women and power, and women and children make a good basis for discussion of the role of contemporary women too. Henrietta Leyser explains the limited lot of Medieval women and poses good questions about their lifestyles.

244
MOSS, Miriam
Traditional Costume
Wayland
1988 £5.95 32pp
1 85210 101 6

This is an intelligent introduction to costumes from around the world. Miriam Moss gives a brief explanation of the different materials which are used around the world and why costumes have developed to suit particular cultural or climatic needs before she gives details of what is worn in each country.

245
PETTENUZZO, Brenda
I Have Cerebral Palsy
photographs by Chris Fairclough
Franklin Watts
1988 £5.25 32pp
0 86313 699 0

Maria Hill has cerebral palsy. This book shows how Maria lives and how many things she does like any other eight-year-old, as well as the different things she has to do in order to counter the effects caused by her condition. The success of *I Have Cerebral Palsy* lies in the fact that Brenda Pettenuzzo's text concentrates on Maria as a person as well as giving a great deal of detailed information about the various causes of cerebral palsy and the treatments of it.

246
PETTY, Kate
Staying Overnight
illustrated by Lisa Kopper
Franklin Watts
1988 £3.95 18pp
0 86313 677 X

Staying Overnight is an attractive picture book story with a message. Sam's experiences of staying his first night away from home will reassure children about doing the same thing themselves. Kate Petty covers some of the difficulties which may occur, like food that you don't like or a night fright you can't handle. Lisa Kopper's illustrations make the story fun and reassuring too.

247
POSTGATE, Oliver
LINNELL, Naomi
Becket
Kingfisher
1989 £6.95 40pp
0 86272 405 8

Becket is a visual treat as well as a highly entertaining way of finding out all about the life and times of Thomas à Becket, the Archbishop of Canterbury who was murdered in his own cathedral on the instructions of King Henry II. The story is told through a continuous strip illustration, in the style of the period, with explanations in the chatty and highly readable text which runs below. The pictures are full of tiny details which make you look and look again. A fuller rendering of the story, interpreting it as a personal struggle between two powerful individuals rather than as a battle between church and state, is given at the end.

248
RICKARD, Graham
The Chernobyl
Catastrophe
illustrated by Peter Bull
Wayland
1988 £5.75 32pp
1 85210 428 7

Graham Rickard tells the story of the terrible disaster at Chernobyl vividly. He studies how it happened, the effect it had on the surrounding countryside and the effect it had on the rest of Europe; he looks at who was to blame and whether such a thing could happen again. The study of this catastrophe makes a provoking starting point for thinking about the issue of nuclear energy in general.

249
ROSS, Stewart
The First World War
Wayland
1989 £8.95 72pp
1 85210 796 0

The use of excellent photographs, diagrams and maps makes this wide ranging account of many different aspects of the First World War vivid and comprehensible. The text gives a brief account of the chain of events leading up to the war, describes some of the action and looks at the impact the war had on civilians.

250
SANDERS, Pete
On the Road
Franklin Watts
1989 £6.50 32pp
0 86313 788 1

Though not especially well laid out, this contains lots of reinforcing information about how to be safe on the road, or by the road, in all sorts of circumstances. Whether playing or travelling, children need to understand the danger that lies in the speed at which cars travel. Good photographs show children exactly what to do and not to do.

251
SHAMIR, Ilana (editor)
SHAVIT, Shlomo (editor)
The Young Reader's
Encyclopedia of Jewish
History
Viking Kestrel
1988 £8.95 126pp
0 670 81738 4

Highly illustrated from a vast range of sources - cartoons, pictures, photographs, maps and diagrams - *The Young Reader's Encyclopedia of Jewish History* is an extremely approachable source of concise information about the different important moments in Jewish history. Beginning at the beginning with the emergence of the Jewish nation made up from an amalgamation of previously nomadic tribes, it follows the spreading of Judaism throughout the world and the subsequent persecution of Jews in different countries at different times. The concluding chapters look at how Jewish people live today and trace the history of Jerusalem through the ages.

252
SHERWIN, Jane
Human Rights
Wayland
1989 £6.95 48pp
1 85210 435 X

Jane Sherwin's text is both well informed and impassioned. She has selected photographs which make her points horribly forcefully. Throughout the world and throughout history, up to and including the present day, the struggle for human rights has gone on. This book looks in detail at some of those particular struggles as well as considering the broader implications of the philosophy of human rights and the role which certain individuals have played.

253
SHILEGER, Maria
(selector)
Prayers For Children
illustrated by Inga Moore
Kingfisher
1988 £5.95 58pp
0 86272 310 8

This is an interestingly broad collection of prayers taken from all around the world. There are prayers for every occasion, mood or situation reflecting the many different ways in which we may need or seek help.

254
STEWART, Anne
The Park Warden
photographs by Chris
Fairclough
Hamish Hamilton
1988 £4.95 32pp
0 241 12218 X

The Park Warden describes a way of life suitable only for the very fit. Sam Roberts is a Warden in the Snowdonia National Park and it is on the slopes of Snowdon itself that he spends most of his time. This book gives a vivid account of the different things he may do in a day's work. There's helping walkers keep safe on the mountain, maintaining fences and paths, rescuing sheep and sometimes rescuing people too. Chris Fairclough's photographs give a clear impression of what the work and the environment are like.

255
STONE, Susheila
Eid ul-Fitr
photographs by
Prodeepta
Das
A. & C. Black
1988 £4.50 32pp
0 7136 3054 X

Through text and photographs Susheila Stone tells how the festival of Eid is celebrated by some Muslims in this country. The practice of fasting, giving and receiving presents, getting new clothes and attending mosque are all described as they effect Fozia and her brother Rehan. There is little explanation of the reasons for and traditions behind the celebrations in the main text, though there is a brief section on further reading about Islam at the end of the book.

256
STONES, Rosemary
Getting to Know London
illustrated by Sharon
Scotland
Dinosaur
1989 £1.95 24pp
0 85122 763 5 P

Easy to read and fun to look at, this is an excellent first introduction to London. Rosemary Stones has picked out the major sites - the British Museum, the Houses of Parliament, St. Paul's Cathedral, Hyde Park, Piccadilly Circus - and described them concisely, giving their historical background as well as the main things to look for.

257
THOMPSON, Ruth
and Neil
The Perfect Present
A. & C. Black
1989 £4.50 25pp
0 7136 3063 9

The story of Okolo's search for a present for his Aunty Vera is set in Barbados. The storyline will be familiar to children everywhere but in reading this they will also find out much about life in Barbados - the difference between the countryside and the big town; how many of the things in the shops are the same as what we have at home; how beautiful the beaches are and how Christmas is celebrated with sparkling lights and a tree - and sorrel juice. Text and photographs are well matched; both make their points without the need for explanation.

258
VAUGHAN, Jenny
Bank
Macmillan
1989 £6.95 48pp
0 333 45973 3

In a series of clearly laid out double spreads, *Bank* covers a vast range of information about all the different things that banks do. Starting by giving an historical and geographical context for the banking we know about, it goes on to describe a local bank, what it does and how, from passing cash over the counter to lending money for expanding businesses. It describes world banking, briefly, and then gives some idea of what it might be like to work in a bank.

259
WARNOCK, Kitty
Mary Wollstonecraft
Hamish Hamilton
1988 £5.95 64pp
0 241 12151 5

Mary Wollstonecraft has often been called the first feminist and Kitty Warnock's readable biography of her explains exactly why she deserves that title. Born in 1759 Mary Wollstonecraft was always conscious of the second rate way in which women were treated and she was determined to fight against it. In an age when women were offered few choices, Mary consistently broke the rules of convention. She hated social injustice of any kind and was convinced that women should have the same rights - to education, employment and the vote - as men. Kitty Warnock traces the ups and downs of her life, giving meaning to it by setting it firmly in its historical context.

260
WILLIAMSON, David
The Third Reich
Wayland
1989 £6.95 64pp
1 85210 321 3

David Williamson explains clearly the reasons for the downfall of the Weimar Republic before giving a lucid account of Hitler's rise to power and the establishment of the Third Reich. The text is detailed but easy to read and the use of a wealth of visual materials - photographs, cartoons, posters - as well as quotes taken from original sources such as speeches and documents give the subject authenticity and immediacy.

261
WOOD, Jenny
Jewish
photographs by Chris Fairclough
Franklin Watts
1988 £5.25 32pp
0 86313 670 2

Jewish is an introductory look at how Jewish families celebrate their culture as individual families and communally. The text is simple and brief. Most of the information can be learnt from the photographs which excellently capture the different moods of the different occasions.

262
WOOD, Tim
Truck Driver
photographs by Chris Fairclough
Franklin Watts
1989 £5.50 32pp
0 86313 822 5

A very brief, clearly printed and easy-to-read text is used to describe a truck driver's trip to collect a load of yoghurt from Belgium. Aspects of the journey, the loading and the unloading, and the moments of rest and relaxation are all described in the text and reflected in the bold, informative photographs.

LIVING WORLD

Endangered species, common insects, animals for pets - all of these are covered in the books that follow. Some of the books are for reference, some for reading and some form the basis of experimental work in the classroom or at home.

263
BAILEY, Jill
Mimicry and Camouflage
Hodder & Stoughton
1988 £6.95 64pp
0 340 42660 8

The degree to which animals, insects and plants can change colour and shape in self-defence is extraordinary. In many cases you have to look carefully at the illustrations to be able to detect the hidden creature. Jill Bailey's comprehensible text explains how the camouflage is achieved and why it is necessary. Her descriptions are full of detailed information without being indigestible.

264
BENDER, Lionel
Poisonous Insects
Franklin Watts
1988 £5.95 32pp
0 86313 764 4

Fortunately for us most of the ten poisonous insects in this book are harmful to other insects or to plants rather than to humans. The act of poisoning of each of these insects is recorded in a colour photograph while the short text describes how the poison is produced and secreted and what effect it has on its victim. *Poisonous Insects* makes a strong impact and is a good, if brief, introduction to the subject.

265
BIRKHEAD, Mike
The Kestrel in the Town
photographs by Oxford
Scientific Films
Methuen
1988 £5.95 32pp
0 416 06552 X

Kestrels have adapted easily and completely to living in towns. The brilliant photographs in this book show kestrels perching happily on drainpipes and old lumps of metal and laying eggs on a window ledge. There is plenty of prey for them in towns as an action shot of a kestrel snatching a redstart chick from the nest well shows. Mike Birkhead's text is both enormously readable and tells you everything you want to know about the subject.

266
BUTTERWORTH,
Christine
Eagles
Macmillan
1989 £5.95 32pp
0 333 48666 8

A simple, first introduction to a noble bird. *Eagles* describes how the birds live, how they court, nest and bring up their young. Information is offered in a descriptive text rather than in fact form and there is no index. Good action photographs show an eagle hunting down a rabbit and a sea eagle swooping down on a fish and plucking it from the sea.

267
DIXON, Annabelle
Wool
photographs by Ed
Barber
A. & C. Black
1989 £4.50 25pp
0 7136 3049 3

Wool, from the sheep to the back, how it is sheared, washed, dyed, carded, knitted and woven is all explained in *Wool*. Annabelle Dixon describes the various stages in clear terms and Ed Barber's photographs show children trying out some of the stages for themselves. The practical advice and applications make the pure information easy to understand.

268
FITZGERALD, Janet
Spring on the Farm
Hamish Hamilton
1989 £6.50 32pp
0 241 12580 4

Springtime on a farm is always a time of great changes. New grass is beginning to grow and it is warm enough for baby animals to survive out of doors. Chicks, ducklings, baby birds and lambs are all born. All this is shown in the photographs which are accompanied by questions which will encourage children to look closely at the changes in the countryside and to understand how and why they come about.

269
GOODALL, Jane
The Chimpanzee Family
Book
photographs by Michael
Neugebauer
Picture Book Studio
1989 £7.95 60pp
0 88708 090 1

Jane Goodall has studied this group of chimpanzees over many years, and knows them intimately. Here she describes their daily family life to us. She can recognise their different moods and these are well reflected in Michael Neugebauer's photographs which show the chimpanzees as they play, feed, groom themselves and finally settle for bed.

270
HENWOOD, Chris
Frogs
photographs by Barrie
Watts
Franklin Watts
1988 £5.25 32pp
0 86313 693 1

Although frogspawn can be collected free from ponds and ditches, frogs need care and atten tion if they are to survive in captivity. The simple text and clear photographs in this book show well how to look after frogs, the kind of habitat and food they need and, most importantly, how they should be handled.

271
JOLY, Dominique
All About Salt
illustrated by Sylvaine
Perols
Moonlight
1988 £2.95 36pp
1 85103 036 0

This attractive book contains a mass of information about salt - where it comes from, how it is gathered, what effects it has, what its uses are. The illustrations are pretty but also accurate, matching well the chatty style of the text.

272
McGAVIN, George
Discovering Bugs
illustrated by Wendy
Medway
Nayland
1988 £5.50 48pp
1 85210 065 6

Bugs, for the most part, are seen as pests rather than friends but this book shows them in their best light and gives an indication of just how interesting they are. As there are about 67,000 different kinds of bug *Discovering Bugs* can only touch on a few of them but it gives details of the main features of a bug, some of the common shapes and sizes, where bugs live, their life cycle and their defences. The illustrations illuminate the text well and there is a substantial index.

273
MERCER, Ian
Oils
Franklin Watts
1988 £5.95 32pp
0 86313 770 9

Oils are found in such a remarkable range of sources and used in so many different ways that it is hard to see how they all come to be called by the same name. *Oils* gives a brief account of oils from plants and animals and how they are extracted, and oils from the ground and how they are refined and then used.

274
PLUCKROSE, Henry
Look at Fur and Feathers
Franklin Watts
1989 £5.95 32pp
0 86313 831 4

The simple text and clear photographs explain the uses of fur and feathers. Owls' feathers, for example, are especially soft so that they can fly silently. Badgers, with their poor eyesight, need to be strongly marked so that they can recognise one another. A brief section at the end gives suggestions for making things with feathers as well as some common sayings which incorporate fur or feather.

275
POPE, Joyce
Kenneth Lilly's Animals
illustrated by Kenneth Lilly
Walker
1988 £12.95 96pp
0 7445 0604 2

Kenneth Lilly's illustrations are exquisite, combining beauty and accuracy perfectly. In this 'portfolio of paintings' he shows the animals of different habitats - Hot Forests, Cool Forests, Seas and Rivers, Grasslands, Deserts and Mountains. The brief text accompanying the illustrations gives extremely readable information about the lifestyle of each animal.

276
ROWAN, Peter
Never Shave a Camel
illustrated by Maggie Ling
Cape
1988 £4.95 96pp
0 224 02607 0

Never Shave a Camel is an extremely successful blend of amusing anecdotes and useful facts for how to deal with surprising and unexpected occurrences. 'What happens if you fall into shark-infested water?' You may just be eaten alive but there are many who have encountered sharks and lived to tell the tale. Peter Rowan gives some explanations of the whys and wherefores of sharks eating men. 'What happens if a centipede crawls up your nose?' Perhaps the thought is too horrific to contemplate, on the other hand if you read this book you will at least know what to do.

277
ROWLAND-
ENTWISTLE,
Theodore
Focus on Silk
Wayland
1988 £6.50 48pp
1 85210 072 9

Silk is produced by all kinds of insects and by spiders. It has the most remarkable properties, most notably that it is three times stronger than a steel thread of the same weight. *Focus on Silk* is a comprehensive account of the discovery of silk; the life story of the silk worm and how they are bred specifically for harvesting the silk; collecting, spinning and weaving silk; and finally the uses of silk in society. Good photographs match this extremely informative text well.

278
SPROULE, Anna
SPROULE, Michael
Know your Pet - Gerbils
Wayland
1988 £6.95 48pp
1 85210 372 8

Before taking on a pet, or choosing the one most suitable for you, you need to know quite a lot about them. Anna and Michael Sproule give masses of information about the right kind of cage and how gerbils need a place to play, about cleaning the cage and grooming the animal and even, if you become really dedicated, about showing gerbils. There are plenty of good photographs to illustrate the text which is aimed directly at future gerbil owners.

279
SYMES, R.F.
Rock and Mineral
Dorling Kindersley
1988 £6.95 64pp
0 86318 273 9

Excellent photographs of large chunks of the rocks in question make this both an attractive and an easy-to-use reference guide. There is some brief background information about the Earth and how particular rock formations have occurred. The different rocks - such as igneous and sedimentary - are described in more detail, as are some of the stones, metals and minerals that are found in them. The practicalities of collecting rocks and minerals, what equipment is needed and how to set about it, are clearly explained too.

280
WATTS, Barrie
Dragonfly
A. & C. Black
1988 £4.50 32pp
0 7136 3053 1

One of the 'Stopwatch' series, *Dragonfly* tells the story of the dragonfly moment by moment, from egg to fully fledged adult in beautiful, clear photographs. The text describes and explains what is happening in the pictures and how the whole process works.

The world of science and technology is changing so fast that it is vital to keep up to date with the new information that is constantly being made available. From very early on children are curious about how and why things work - whether in the unfamiliar world of space or on the more domestic level in the kitchen.

281
CRAIG, Annabel
ROSNEY, Cliff
The Usborne Science Encyclopedia
illustrated by Chris Byon
illustrated by John Shackell
illustrated by Ian Jackson
Usborne
1988 £7.95 128pp
0 7460 0192 4

Divided into categories of Counting and Measuring, Heat and Energy, Forces and Machines, Light and Colour, Sound and Hearing, Atoms and Molecules, Electricity and Technology, this is a good introduction to some of the scientific explanations of the world around us. The explanations are simple, sometimes over simplified, and the points made are reinforced by good diagrams and comic cartoons. Lists, tables, a glossary and a comprehensive index make this book especially useful.

282
GRAHAM, Ian
Submarines
Franklin Watts
1989 £6.50 32pp
0 86313 936 1

Ian Graham gives a moderately detailed technical account of how submarines work and of the work they do. Diagrams and photographs help to illuminate the text and a glossary provides help with the unfamiliar vocabulary.

283
HATCHETT, Clint
The Glow in the Dark Night Sky Book
illustrated by Stephen Marchesi
Heinemann
1989 £5.95 19pp
0 434 94224 3

Though apparently slightly gimmicky with its star maps that glow in the dark after brief exposure to light, this is a genuinely useful aid for all those who want to learn what to look for when they look at the stars. Heather Couper has provided an admirable introduction which explains exactly how to use the book and what to look for in the sky itself, while a brief glossary at the end of the book explains the meaning of the constellations' names.

284
JENNINGS, Terry
Sliding and Rolling
illustrated by David
Anstey
Oxford
1989 £3.50 24pp
0 19 918272 8

The simple principles behind rolling and sliding are introduced in a chatty, story style. Why does the lorry roll further when the slope is steeper? William is on ice skates and Anna is on roller skates. Which is sliding and which is rolling? Simple experiments are included in the text making the book useful for using with a class as well as fun for children to manage on their own.

285
LAMBERT, Mark
Twentieth Century
Communications
Wayland
1988 £6.95 48pp
1 85210 315 9

Mark Lambert traces the history of radio, television, radar and computers, giving a good historical perspective to things that we nowadays take for granted. His extensive use of photographs forcefully brings home just how dramatic and how quick the changes in these fields have been.

286
MACAULAY, David
The Way Things Work
Dorling Kindersley
1988 £15 384pp
0 86318 323 9

This is a massive and comprehensive guide to the world of machines and how they work. It is intelligently divided into four thematic chapters. 'The Mechanics of Movement' explains levers, wheels, gears, pulleys and cranes; 'Harnessing the Elements' looks at floating, flying, exploiting heat and nuclear power ; 'Working With Waves' shows how light waves and sound waves are used in mechanical processes and 'Electricity and Automation' studies electricity and magnetism as well as giving a clear account of computers and how they work. Each principle is explained and its working is then applied to a familiar process - lawnmowers, pneumatic drills, car suspension and the like. *The Way Things Work* offers a wealth of extremely complicated information at a high level. Its logical text and well-labelled diagrams make it nonetheless extraordinarily comprehensible.

LEVERS

*I*t was then that I noticed across the square a second equally large mammoth about to be weighed, this time using far fewer people as a counterbalance. As I watched, anticipating disaster, the boulder was rolled closer to what would be the mammoth's end of the tree trunk. Once the mammoth was in place, a mere handful of people climbed onto the other end. To my amazement the tree trunk gently assumed a horizontal position. I was then informed that the length of the tree trunk from the people to the boulder multiplied by their combined weight would equal the length of the trunk from the boulder to the mammoth multiplied by its weight.

I was in the midst of calculations to verify this most unlikely theory when I heard a scream. Apparently, all the villagers had not disembarked from the trunk simultaneously, thereby causing a lad to be dramatically launched. I made a note, thinking that one day this might be useful.

FIRST-CLASS LEVERS

There are three different basic kinds of levers. All the levers on these two pages are first-class levers. First-class levers aren't superior to other-class levers, they are just levers in which the fulcrum is always placed between the effort and the load.

If the fulcrum is placed in the centre – as in the diagram on the left – the effort and load are at the same distance from it and are equal. The weight of the people is the same as the weight of the mammoth.

However, if the people are placed twice as far from the fulcrum as the mammoth – as in the diagram on the right – only half the number of people is needed to raise the mammoth. And if the people were three times as far from the fulcrum than the mammoth, only a third would be needed, and so on, because the lever magnifies the force applied to it. These mammoth-weighing levers balance in order to measure weight, which is why this kind of weighing machine is called a balance. When the lever comes to rest, the force of the effort balances the force of the load, which is its weight. Many other kinds of levers work to produce movement.

FULCRUM OFF-CENTRE
The effort is twice as far from the fulcrum as the load. Here, the effort moves twice as far as the load, but is only half its amount.

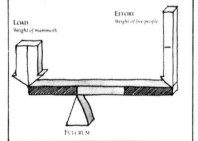

LOAD
Weight of mammoth

EFFORT
Weight of five people

FULCRUM

287
NEWSON, Lesley
Dealing With Dirt
illustrated by Chris
Masters
A. & C. Black
1989 £4.95 64pp
0 7136 3046 9

Subtitled 'The Science of Cleaning' this takes a
look at what dirt is, and what the detergents
that treat it are, in scientific terms. The text is
serious and packed full of facts, and the il
lustrations are witty, a combination that makes
the subject extremely approachable and easy
to follow.

288
PRUNIER, James
The Story of Trains
illustrated by James
Prunier
translated by Sarah
Matthews
Moonlight
1988 £4.95 96pp
1 85103 047 6

This pocket-sized book is stuffed full of
train information of all kinds. The technical
developments of wheels, rails, steam power
tunnelling and bridge building are all covered
as well as the technologies of present-day
trains, such as the Japanese Bullet Train and
the new high-speed trains in Europe. There is
social history too, in the accounts of how
railways developed differently in the different
countries of the world. The author's en
thusiasm for his subject is apparent in both
text and pictures.

289
RICHARDSON, Joy
Turn on a Tap
illustrated by
Sue Barclay and
Dee McLean
Hamish Hamilton
1988 £5.95 32pp
0 241 12086 1

A simple text and good diagrammatic illustra
tions make this an easy-to-follow introduction
to the mysteries of how the water we get out
of a tap gets into it in the first place. The
natural process of collecting rain and the
technical process of treating it and piping it
to individual houses are clearly described
Simple, home-based experiments to put the
theory into practice on a small scale are given
too.

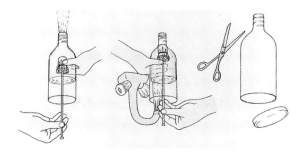

90
ZBROVA, Zuza
Space and Astronomy
Franklin Watts
1989 £6.50 40pp
86313 757 1

Divided into four main sections - The Exploding Universe, The Solar System, Space Science and Mapping the Stars - *Space and Astronomy* is a densely packed, high level account of the world of space and how it has been explored.

91
WHYMAN, Kathryn
Sparks to Power Stations
Franklin Watts
1989 £6.50 32pp
86313 931 0

The title of this book describes exactly what it contains. From the first sparks that come with static electricity in our clothes, through the charges from a battery, conducting and insulating, different types of circuits and on to electromagnets, electrolysis, power stations and how electricity is used in our homes are all explained. But there is more to the book than just theory. Simple experiments with batteries, using a motor as a generator, instructions on how to make a dimmer switch and much more will give children a chance to experience electricity in practice.

Creative and recreational skills need encouragement. The books in this section have been selected to show just how much enthusiasm and initial information can be learnt and then put into practice.

292
BARRETT Norman
Gymnastics
Franklin Watts
1989 £5.25 32pp
0 86313 680 X

This photographic record of gymnastics shows what it looks like at competition level. The simple text explains the photographs - which event, what it involves and how it is marked There is a glossary to elaborate on the technical terms and a brief history of the sport.

293
BIGGS, Jonathan
HORWOOD, Janet
Riding in Motion
illustrated by Richard
Clifton-Dey
Simon & Schuster
1988 £7.95 14pp
0 671 69901 6

The three-dimensional format of this book seems gimmicky but the pop-up illustrations are helpful in clarifying the details of the text as well as making the whole thing seem especially real. Very much a book for those just embarking on being pony mad, *Riding in Motion* covers caring for your pony and the first steps in learning to ride it.

294
COLEMAN, Anne
Fabrics and Yarns
illustrated by Malcolm
S. Walker
Wayland
1989 £5.95 32pp
1 85210 674 3

Weaving, embroidery, appliqué and fabric collage are just some of the areas for creative fun in this helpful, easy-to-follow introduction to a craft project. Anne Coleman gives simple instructions to each section as well as lots of ideas for what to make once the technique has been mastered.

295
CUMMING, David
Photography
Wayland
1989 £7.50 48pp
1 85210 455 4

Photography is a combination of an historical account of the subject and an explanation of it as an art form. The long text recounts the important stages in the development of photography from its early days right up to the present where sophisticated technology has made so many new things possible. Glossy photographs illuminate the points while also reinforcing the argument that photography is an art form.

296
EAST, Helen (compiler)
The Singing Sack
Illustrated by Mary
Currie
A. & C. Black
1989 £7.95 80pp
0 7136 3115 5

Helen East has gathered together twenty-eight very short stories from around the world, each of which contains a dramatic song which children can join in. The result is an exceptionally rich source of songs which are firmly set in their own context.

297
GREEN, Christine
Hair and Make-up
Wayland
1989 £5.95 32pp
1 85210 380 9

Hair and skin - what different kinds there are and what you can do for them - are extensively covered by this book. The emphasis is more on looking after hair and skin and treating them well in a fashionable way, than on being outrageously creative at their expense.

298
Ladybird Dictionary
Illustrated by Mike
Nicholls and Judith Wood
Ladybird
1989 £1.99 187pp
0 7214 7533 7

With each entry in bold type well set out on the page, with a clear definition given in a smaller type face, this is an easy-to-use first dictionary. There are almost four thousand words included, from the obvious to some which will help to expand a vocabulary. The identification of nouns, verbs, prepositions and the rest is especially valuable.

299
LILLEGARD, Dee
Brass
Franklin Watts
1989 £5.95 32pp
0 516 02218 0

The simple, easy-to-follow text of *Brass* describes how you blow a brass instrument, how you use the keys, a mute and a slide and then how the different instruments sound. Action photographs of the instruments being played bring the text to life.

300
MANN, Brenda
Cinema in the
Twentieth Century
Wayland
1989 £6.95 48pp
1 85210 399 X

Brenda Mann gives a straightforward history of the cinema from the 1890s when photographic pioneers were scrambling to be first with a technique for showing moving pictures, to the present day with its highly sophisticated technology and 'mega bucks' film industry. What can be done in the cinema has changed extraordinarily in a short time as the photographs included in *Cinema* show. They also reflect the rapidly changing tastes of the cinema-going public.

301
PEACH, Susan
Improve Your Running
Skills
Usborne
1988 £3.95 48pp
0 7460 0166 5

This is a serious and invaluable handbook for those who are serious about running. Every aspect of training, equipment and race tactics is covered in short sections of text. Illustrations illuminate the points made, making it easy to understand all the technicalities of the sport.

302
PETTY, Kate
Cats
Franklin Watts
1988 £5.25 24pp
0 86313 798 9

Largely a selection of dramatic pictures showing different cats doing different things, *Cats* is a good introduction to how cats behave naturally and how they behave and can be cared for domestically.

303
PINDER, Steve
STEEN, Robert
Sportswatching
illustrated by
G.J. Galsworthy
Puffin
1988 £1.99 224pp
0 14 032617 0 P

Bowls, cycling, cricket, darts, ice hockey, squash - this is an excellent introduction to the salient features of each of thirty-two sports which you may be watching on television. Each sport is given a general introduction and a brief history before the details of tactics and equipment are explained. Clear, diagrammatic illustrations illuminate precise details - like which cricket fielder is which. Though full of facts, *Sportswatching* remains easy and fun to read.

304
THOMPSON, Brian
PUFFIN First Picture
Dictionary
illustrated by Celia
Berridge
Puffin
1988 £2.99 48pp
0 14 050777 9 P

Clear and bright illustrations and a careful selection of words make this an extremely useful word guide for children who are just beginning to read, write and spell on their own.

305
UMANSKY, Kaye
Phantasmagoria
illustrated by Chris
Smedley
A. & C. Black
1988 £6.95 64pp
0 7136 3072 8

Divided into three sections - 'The Magic Canoe', 'Flight of the Starship Silver Grey' and 'A Night in Spooksville' - this is a collection of exciting songs which can just be played or which can be used as a starting point for an interesting exploration of sounds. There are masses of dramatic actions to accompany each song which make the actual verses especially vivid.

306
VAN ZANDT, Eleanor
Dance
Wayland
1988 £7.50 48pp
1 85210 342 6

Starting with the claim that dance is the oldest of all the arts, *Dance* studies the origins of dance all over the world and looks at how it has evolved into the formalised art form it is today. The text is full of technical information but remains readable. It is supported by attractive photographs which show just how much scope there is in dance.

307
WOOD, Tim
Spotlight on Flags
Franklin Watts
1989 £5.95 32pp
0 86313 801 2

Today flags are little more than attractive decoration but in the past their importance was great as a single language, long-range method of communication. *Spotlight on Flags* gives a brief account of the historic importance of flags as well as providing a small coloured image of the present-day flags of each country.

308
WRIGHT, Lyndie
Puppets
photographs by Chris Fairclough
Franklin Watts
1988 £6.95 48pp
0 86313 743 1

With the minimum amount of fuss puppets can give children the chance to be all kinds of characters. *Puppets* describes how to make the simplest puppets to use - painted fingers or hands; simple glove puppets; wooden spoon puppets; *papier mâché* glove puppets and the more sophisticated puppets with strings. A brief history of puppets and a list of the best puppet museums are also included. Lyndie Wright's clear text and Chris Fairclough's attractive photographs make this an excellent introduction to the subject.

INDEX OF AUTHORS AND ILLUSTRATORS

INDEX OF TITLES

Wayland

21 good reasons for Wayland

Wayland, one of the world's leading publishers of entertaining and stimulating information books, celebrates its 21st Birthday next year. What could be better to mark the occasion than having 21 of its titles selected for the 1989 Children's Books of the Year selection.

All carefully written and colourfully illustrated, 1200 titles in over 100 series cover broad subject areas including History, Geography, Science, Nature and Social Studies. Always ready to reflect current concerns, Wayland's absorbing new Ecology, Conservation and Energy series will be of particular interest to teachers, librarians and readers alike.

Wayland's 21 Children's Books of the Year 1989

Wayland (Publishers) Ltd. and Firefly Books Ltd.

celebrate an early birthday

Firefly

This year Wayland was proud to announce the launching of an exciting new range of books for younger children.

Firefly Books satisfy the growing demand for elementary non-fiction or 3-8 year olds, aimed at bridging the gap between traditional picture books and nior information books.

or full information on Wayland and Firefly books, contact our Sales Departments now.

61 Western Road, Hove, East Sussex BN3 1JD, England.
Tel: (0273) 722561. Fax: (0273) 29314. Telex: 878170

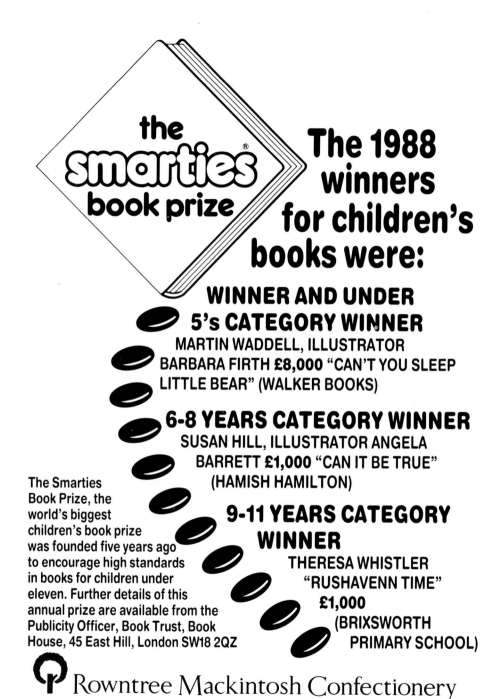

BEST BOOKS FOR BEDTIME FROM
WALKER

Can't You Sleep, Little Bear?
Written by Martin Waddell
and illustrated by Barbara Firth
£6.95   0-7445-0796-0

Winner of the
1988 Smarties Grand Prize
and the
1988 Kate Greenaway Medal

NOW
From the same award-winning
combination of author and
illustrator comes

The Park in the Dark
£6.95   0-7445-0716-2

Books for Keeps said of
The Park in the Dark
"Remember *Can't You Sleep, Little Bear?*
Who could forget it? As one of the best picture
books of 1988, it became at once an almost
Impossible Act to Follow in 1989, even by this
hugely talented pair. So let it be said at the
outset that this book isn't of the same quality…
in my view it's even better."

YOUNG WATERSTONE'S

Young Waterstone's is a bookshop specially for children with over 50,000 books to cater for all ages from pre-school to young adult.

It's also a stationery shop – with all sorts of things like paper, crayons, pens, paints, things for school, tapes and activity toys.

Our staff are happy to help on reading choices and we helpfully keep the shop open until 7 in the evening.

There are reading areas to investigate your favourite books and activities for you to join in – everything from collage workshops to storytelling and joke competitions.

And because children (and their parents) will want to stay a long time in this fairy tale bookshop there are play areas for younger children, special children's toilets and a changing room for babies.

Young Waterstone's is a wonderland for children. 'Please come and visit us.

For details of a Young Waterstone's near you contact our Head Office at
101 Wigmore Street, London, W1H 9AB Telephone 01-499 4999

Don't settle for anything less than the absolute best.

HAMISH HAMILTON CHILDREN'S BOOKS

Hamish Hamilton Children's Books offer a comprehensive list of superb quality titles across all age ranges and subjects, from Non-Fiction to Picture Books, a strong Fiction list and successful beginner readers' series.

Look out this Autumn for new titles by top authors and illustrators:

ANTHONY BROWNE   A Bear-y Tale
BABETTE COLE   Cupid
ERIC CARLE   Have You Seen My Cat? (Mini edition)
SUSAN HILL   Suzy's Shoes
ANDREW & PAULA MARTYR   The Magic Hiccup
TESSA DAHL   Gwenda And The Animals
RUSSELL HOBAN   jim Hedgehog's
Supernatural Christmas
JOAN LINGARD   Tug Of War
ROBERT SWINDELLS   Follow A Shadow
LOIS DUNCAN   Don't Look Behind You

Also many new additions to our popular Non-Fiction series

HAMISH HAMILTON CHILDREN'S BOOKS
(9 out of 10 cats prefer them!)

Wheeee!

The Goodger and friends have made it... into Childrens Books of the year 1989

(AN IMAGINARY MENAGERIE by Roger McGough, illustrated by Tony Ross)

So have many more top-quality titles from

Viking Kestrel

Picture Books
STARTING SCHOOL Janet & Allan Ahlberg
MOUSETALE Margaret Gordon
TEDDY BEAR BOATMAN Phoebe Worthington
CATCH IT IF YOU CAN Brian Thompson/Susie Jenkin-Pearce
MRS JOLLY'S JOKE SHOP Allan Ahlberg/Colin McNaughton

Young Fiction
THE LITTLE EXPLORER Margaret Joy
RIDE TO THE RESCUE June Crebbin
TALES FROM THE SHOP THAT NEVER SHUTS Martin Waddell

Poetry
AN IMAGINARY MENAGERIE Roger McGough/Tony Ross
EVERY POEM TELLS A STORY Raymond Wilson

Fiction
THE EMPTY SLEEVE Leon Garfield
STAN Ann Pilling

Non-Fiction
YOUNG READER'S ENCYCLOPEDIA
O F JEWISH HISTORY Shamir/Shavit

Kestrel Teenage Trade Paperbacks
BIANCA Joan Phipson
DOUBLE TAKE June Oldham
THE GIRL Robbie Branscum
RUNNING RIOT John Kenworthy
SHOWDOWN Jon Blake

The best from Heinemann...

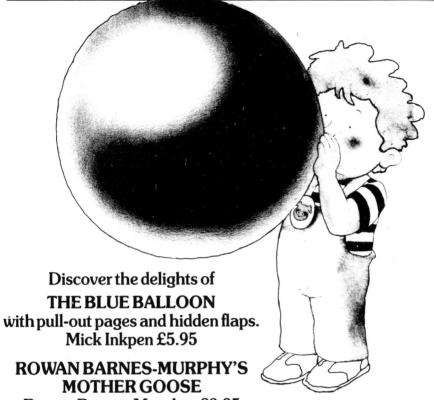

Janet and Allan Ahlberg · Bernard Ashley ·

Nina Bawden · Quentin Blake · Eric Carle ·

PUFFIN

Helen Cresswell · Roald Dahl · Hunter Davies ·

HAS

Anne Fine · Michael Foreman · Eric Hill ·

A CHOICE

Colin and Jaqui Hawkins · Shirley Hughes ·

OF BOOKS

Pat Hutchins · Terry Jones · Dick King-Smith ·

for every day,

Gene Kemp · Joan Lingard · Penelope Lively ·

of every week,

Jan Mark · Roger McGough · Philippa Pearce ·

for every month,

Jill Murphy · Helen Nicoll · Brian Patten ·

of every year...

Ann Pilling · Jan Pieńkowski · Michael Rosen ·

Maurice Sendak · Posy Simmonds · John Rowe

Townsend · Jill Tomlinson · Jill Paton Walsh ·

Robert Westall · Ursula Moray Williams ·

Bob Wilson · Kit

Wright · Tony Ross ·

The Watts Group

Franklin Watts

Orchard Books

Gloucester Press

Campbell Books

Publishers of quality children's books for all ages.

For a catalogue please contact:

Linda Banner, Promotions Manager,
The Watts Group, 96 Leonard Street,
LONDON EC2A 4RH Tel: 01 739 2929

the best from Methuen...

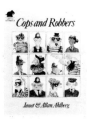

JOIN

The Early Worm Club
0-7 years

The Bookworm Club
7-13 years

ENCOURAGE YOUR CHILDREN TO DISCOVER THE PLEASURE OF BOOKS AND TO DEVELOP THE
READING HABIT

We offer: Two easy to operate Bookclubs: **Early Worm** for all children up to the age of seven and **Bookworm** for seven to thirteen age group.

Full colour leaflets illustrating the range of the best books for children.

Six new selections of books, per club, a year.

10% Cash Bonus on all orders for schools and groups.

Books sent **Post Free** and by return.

Free gifts and posters throughout the year.

ANDERSEN PRESS
Autumn Books

PICTURE BOOKS IN FULL COLOUR

SWAN LAKE
Margot Fonteyn and Trina Schart Hyman
32pp 280 x 254mm
0 86264 238 8 £7.95
September
The legend which became the world's best-loved ballet is magically retold here by Dame Margot Fonteyn with stunning illustrations by Trina Schart Hyman.

DR XARGLE'S BOOK OF EARTH HOUNDS
Jeanne Willis and Tony Ross
32pp 230 x 200mm
0 86264 249 3 £5.95
September
The Doctor teaches his class of aliens about man's best friend. Tony Ross's exuberant pictures and Jeanne Willis's witty text combine once more in the hilarious sequel to *Dr Xargle's Book of Earthlets*, acclaimed by *The Listener.* "Brilliantly funny".

THE MONSTER AND THE TEDDY BEAR
David McKee
32pp 230 x 200mm
0 86264 258 2 £5.95
November
When Angela's wish to have a monster for a playmate comes true, things soon get out of hand. But can Teddy save the day? *Who's a Clever Baby then?* was praised by *The Listener.* "Vintage McKee".

THE KNIGHT WHO WAS AFRAID OF THE DARK
Barbara Shook Hazen and Tony Ross
32pp 267 x 214mm
0 86264 252 3 £6.95
July
Sir Fred is bold – but terrified of the dark! Tony Ross's ebullient pictures capture the flavour of Barbara Hazen's rollicking tale.

THE TREASURE OF COSY COVE
Tony Ross
32pp 240 x 200mm
0 86264 256 6 £5.95
September
Cap'n Claws, the pirate cat, takes Smudge and Kitty on an exciting voyage to discover the treasure of Cosy Cove. Tony's most ambitious book to date will delight adults and children alike.

FROG IN LOVE
Max Velthuijs
Translated by Anthea Bell
32pp 230 x 200mm
0 86264 240 X £5.95
September
"A frog can't be in love with a duck" say his friends, but Frog is determined to win Duck's affection. This enchanting story is the first book for Andersen Press by the award-winning Dutch artist.

TILLIE AND THE WALL
Leo Lionni
32pp 280 x 220mm
0 86264 236 1 £6.95
September
What's on the other side of the wall? Tillie intends to find out. Lionni's wise fable is told in bold, colourful collages. *Nicholas Where Have You Been?* was acclaimed by *Books for Keeps:* "Not to be missed".

PUSS IN PALACE
Frederic and Francoise Joos
English version Paul Sidey
32pp 230 x 200mm
0 86264 235 3 £5.95
November
The charming tale of a pampered cat who lives in a sultan's palace is the second book from Francoise and Frederic Joos.

JOEY'S COMING HOME TODAY

Louis Baum and Susan Varley
32pp 230 x 200mm
0 86264 233 7 £5.95
November

Joey's sister can hardly wait for him to come home from boarding school. Louis Baum's touching story of a child's anticipation of the holidays is sensitively interpreted by Susan Varley.

THE SHINING PRINCESS AND OTHER JAPANESE LEGENDS

Eric Quayle and Michael Foreman
112pp 240 x 184mm
0 86264 236 1 £8.95
September

As a follow-up to their much-praised The Magic Ointment and Other Cornish Legends, Eric Quayle and Michael Foreman have collaborated to create this sumptuous collection of Japanese folk tales.

TIGERS – NEW READ-ALONE FICTION

launched with Century Hutchinson

THROUGH THE WITCH'S WINDOW

Hazel Townson
64pp 198 x 129mm
0 86264 255 8 £3.95
September

When Lily breaks Granny Gowie's window she is pursued by a strange black star. Is the old woman a witch who has put a spell on Lily?

STANLEY MAKES IT BIG

David Tinkler
64pp 198 x 129mm
0 86264 257 4 £3.95
September

When Smudge stops messing up Stanley's schoolwork and starts helping him instead, Stanley's school career takes an amazing and hilarious turn for the better!

ANDERSEN YOUNG READERS' LIBRARY

MR BROWSER MEETS THE MIND SHRINKERS

Philip Curtis
128pp 198 x 129mm
0 86264 261 2 £5.95
October

The twelfth Mr Browser story. "This successful series never fails to entertain... the combination of humorous school story and science fiction is stunning". Junior Bookshelf.

WALNUT WHIRL

Hazel Townson
64pp 80pp 198 x 129mm
0 86264 246 9 £4.95
October

Lenny has discovered a walnut shell in his pocket containing microfilm. Is that why he and Jake are being followed? Another zany adventure in the popular series by Hazel Townson.

THE PIRATE ON THE ROOF

Jo Pestum
128pp 198 x 129mm
0 86264 260 4 £5.95
October

The boring school holidays are transformed when Paul begins a thrilling apprenticeship as a pirate. Gene Kemp on Aunt Thea's Tiger. "a treat... a book with style in every sense of the word".

TIME CHILD

David Tinkler
128pp 198 x 129mm
0 86264 248 5 £5.95
November

When a plane crashes on his farm Tony is miraculously saved – by a boy ghost! The Sunday Times acclaimed The Scourge of the Dinner Ladies for "its terrific energy and unfaltering funniness".

CHILDREN'S BOOKS OF THE YEAR 1989

Edited by Julia Eccleshare
128pp 210 x 145mm
0 86264 262 0 £3.95
October

The authoritative guide to the best children's books of the year, published in association with the Book Trust in October, to coincide with Children's Book Week.

ANDERSEN PRESS 62-65 Chandos Place, London WC2N 4NW

BAKER BOOKS

SUPPLIERS OF CHILDRENS BOOKS
TO
SCHOOLS, LIBRARIES, BOOK TRADE
AND FAMILIES

Extensive stocks of dual and single text
foreign language children's books held
including dual language editions of
the famous 'SPOT' books!

*

The new 7th edition of the successful series of
'READING FOR ENJOYMENT' reading guides
for ages 0-18 available October 1989

*

Library Servicing, Stock Selection Visits,
and Exhibitions can be arranged

*

Write in now for the new
MULTI-LINGUAL CATALOGUE
and details of other services

BAKER BOOKS MANFIELD PARK CRANLEIGH SURREY GU6 8NU
Telephone: (0483) 267888

Music, Mystery and Mirth!

Sing Nowell! 34 favourite carols to sing and play
arranged by Timothy Roberts & Jan Betts
Fed up with balancing a dozen different carol books on your knee? Your troubles are over. All your favourite carols are now collected together in one book; arranged simply in easily sung keys with piano accompaniments and guitar chords.
Words & music spiral bound **£6.95** ☆ *Words only* pbk **£1.50**

Jets
Lively stories for the child who is just beginning to enjoy reading.
each hbk **£3.95**

Albertine, Goose Queen
Michael Morpurgo & Shoo Rayner
Albertine thinks she is safe on her island, but the sneaky fox is swimming nearer . . .

Magic Mash
Peter Firmin
Life gets adventurous for Kevin and his grandad when their lunch starts granting them wishes.

Monty, the dog who wears glasses
Colin West
Monty tries to be helpful but somehow he just can't stay out of trouble.

Weedy Me
Sally Christie & Peter Kavanagh
How can you make your grandad like you when he thinks you're a real disappointment?

Crackers
Funny stories for competent readers aged 7–11.   each hbk **£4.50**

It's a Tough Life
Jeremy Strong
When girls invade his den Tom declares war: but if you can't beat them . . .

The Fwog Pwince the twuth!
Kaye Umansky
The truth behind the fairy tale.

Comets
Adventure and mystery for 9–13s.
hbk **£4.50**

The Ten Pound Note
Antony Lishak
How can three children have come by a ten pound note? The psychological mystery unravels.

*For details of further exciting new books, please write to
A & C Black, 35 Bedford Row, London WC1R 4JH*

A & C Black

WHY DO 7500 SCHOOL BOOKSHOPS CHOOSE BOOKS FOR STUDENTS?

★ Our stock comprises all major paperback publishers giving an enormous yet informed selection of titles supplied at a discount.

★ Enticing promotional material ensures curiosity and stimulates the act of browsing.

★ Encouragement to 'save' is provided by our unique saving scheme.

★ Opening times are tailor-made owing to your own choice of stock being near at hand.

FOR AN ANSWER IN MORE DETAIL
Please contact Customer Services

Books For Students, Bird Road, Heathcote, Warwick CV34 6TB
Telephone: (0926) 314366

BOOKS
FOR STUDENTS

A SPONSORED READING EVENT IN AID OF THE MALCOLM SARGENT CANCER FUND FOR CHILDREN

Readathon is a national sponsored read organised by Books for Students. Its aim is to encourage children to read.

Founded six years ago, a million children last year raised £¾ million.

- All the money raised goes to the Malcolm Sargent Cancer Fund for Children
- Honorary Chairman - Roald Dahl
- An ideal Book Week activity for schools and libraries
- Easy to organise.

READATHON
SUPPORTED BY TY·PHOO

FOR FURTHER DETAILS CONTACT:
The Readathon Office, Books for Students, Bird Road, Heathcote, Warwick, CV34 6TB. Tel: (0926) 314366

Come and see all your favourite characters at the

puffin

CHILDREN'S BOOKSHOP

The brightest bookshops —
the best of children's books.

1 The Market, Covent Garden, WC2.
(01) 379 6465

14 Coppergate, York. (0904) 647174

54/56 Bridlesmithgate, Nottingham.
(0602) 599295

Books, Games, Stationery, Toys
Something for everyone!

Access/Visa/Amex/Diner's Club

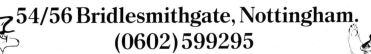

Children's
Book Circle

For people who work
with children's books

•

Monthly meetings

•

Lively discussion

•

Annual conference

Contact:
Caroline Plaisted
01-636 9851

HOW TO FIND THE BOOK ROOM

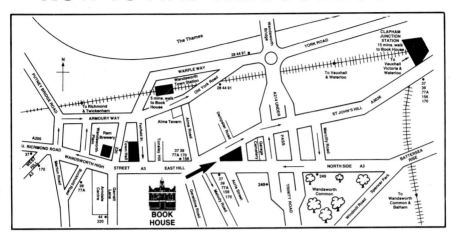

In the Book Room at the **Children's Book Foundation,** Book Trust, you will find the **Children's Books of the Year** and the only comprehensive collection of children's books published over the last two years.

The collection is open to the public and is widely used by teachers, librarians, students, researchers, publishers and others. Its use is not restricted to those professionally concerned with children's books and many parents and children visit regularly.

HOW TO FIND US . ...
FROM CENTRAL LONDON

Waterloo and Vauxhall Station   — Train to Wandsworth Town
  then 5 minute walk.

Victoria Station   — Train to Clapham Junction
  then a bus or 15 minute walk.

Frequent buses to Book House and plenty of free parking space in any of the side roads.

BOOK TRUST

**Book House, 45 East Hill, London SW18-2QZ
Telephone: 01-870 9055**